INSIDE
HEAVEN'S
GATES

A Nineteenth-Century Classic Retold

ISBN-13 978-1-936355-43-3
ISBN-10 1-936355-43-4

Inside Heaven's Gates, originally published as *Intra Muros* in 1898, has been updated for today's reader.

Grace Chapel
3279 Southall Road
Leipers Fork, TN 37064

Cover design: Matt Dolan
Interior design: Bart Dawson

INSIDE HEAVEN'S GATES

A Nineteenth-Century Classic Retold

Rebecca Ruter Springer
(1832–1904)

INTRODUCTION

A Life Changing Book

Welcome to a very special book. This small, yet powerful book radically influenced not only my view of heaven, but also helped me to have a better understanding of how our concept of heaven leads us to live our lives on this earth—with heavenly focus.

My brother Pat introduced me to Rebecca Springer's writing. I told the story in my book *Between Heaven and Earth*. Let me share it here:

About fifteen years ago I received a phone call from my brother Patrick.

I dearly love my older brother and I always welcome his advice and mentoring. I was surprised to hear him weeping on the other end of the phone. He quickly filled me in on what was happening: "Man, I've got a book that I'm reading that is wearing me out. You need to get it."

The book he was talking about was My Dream of Heaven by Rebecca Ruter Springer [retitled from the original Intra Muros by a publisher]. I bought it and read it, and her story floored me. It still floors me today.

Springer's book talks about a spiritual experience she had. First published in 1898 and originally titled Intra Muros, it details Springer's very personal, detailed vision of heaven and gives a beautiful glimpse of the eternal home that awaits us. Billy Graham said that the book "captured biblical truths with emotional impressions."[1]

While reading her story, I had one of those moments in my Christian life when the prospect and reality of heaven became markedly clearer. The book challenged me with concepts I'd never known and provided practical insights that I could share with others who needed help and encouragement.[2]

Why Another One?

While *My Dream of Heaven* is a great book, the more I personally dove into it, used it with other people and gave it away, the more I felt we could go back to the original and make a better edition, that would be more useful in ministry. So, with the help of the Grace Chapel resource team, we did.

- We went back to the original book and brought the language closer to today's, but we also made sure we kept the clarity, distinctiveness, and character of *Intra Muros*.

- We added some valuable resources as an appendix to the book. Rest assured we didn't change the story. It's exactly the same, just written for a modern reader. We added an appendix which gives you some incredibly helpful and biblical insight:

---

1   Billy Graham, *Death and the Life After* (Nashville: W Publishing Group, 1987), 175.
2   Steve Berger, *Between Heaven and Earth: Finding Faith, Hope, Courage and Passion Through a Fresh Vision of Heaven*, (Minneapolis, MN: Baker Publishing Group, 2014).

- ° We added a section about knowing Jesus Christ. We felt it was important to help people actually do this, since going to heaven is centered on knowing Jesus as your personal Savior.
- ° We added two sections of Scripture that help you understand, biblically, what's *not* in heaven and what *is* in heaven. Rebecca Springer's original book gives us a beautifully vivid picture of heaven—now, in the appendix you have the very scriptures that support her writing.
- ° We added a footnote when scripture is spoken in the story. We feel it's important for you to know the scriptures that are within the text of the book.

Thank you for joining us in reading and appreciating Rebecca Springer's book. Once you've read it, I know that it will change your thinking and your life, as it did for me.

God bless you.

Steve Berger, Senior Pastor, Grace Chapel

Leipers Fork, Tennessee

August 2014

AUTHOR'S PREFACE

This is the true, but greatly condensed, record of what I experienced during days when my life hung in the balance between time and eternity.

I am painfully aware that I can never adequately describe the scenes that appeared to me during those days. But if I can show at all how closely linked the two lives—temporal and eternal—appeared to me, I may be able to dispel some of the mystery and fear most of us feel about death, and show it to be simply an open door into a new and beautiful phase of life.

If what I describe seems odd in view of what we've come to expect from the world's view or what we learned in our church, I can only say, "I'm telling it as it came to me." In those strange, happy hours, the close blending of the two lives; the Father's watchful care and tender love; the reunion of friends; the satisfied desires, glad surprises, and divine joys—all intensified by the reverence, love, and adoration that everyone there gave to the blessed Trinity—appeared to me the most perfect revelation of the heaven we dream of.

With the hope that my experience may comfort and uplift some who read it, I offer this imperfect sketch of a most perfect vision.

Rebecca Ruter Springer

CHAPTER 1

I was hundreds of miles from home and friends, and had been very ill for weeks. My only caregiver, though kindhearted, was poorly suited for the job. I had none of the encouragement and care that help speed recovery. I had taken no nourishment of any kind for nearly three weeks, scarcely even water, and was very weak; consciousness seemed at times to wholly desert me. I longed for loved ones who were not with me, needing their gentle touch and words of love and courage; but they never came. Responsibilities that must not be neglected kept them far away much of the time, and I chose not to ask them to come to me.

I lay in a large, comfortable room, on the second floor of a house in Kentville, Canada. The bed stood in a recess at one end of the apartment, near a large stained-glass window that opened to a porch facing the street. During much of my illness I lay facing the window, my back to the room. I remember thinking how easy it would be to pass through the window to the porch.

When the longing for distant faces and voices became more than I could bear, I prayed that Christ would help me feel His presence. Since my earthly loved ones could not be with me, I prayed to feel the influence of the dear servants[3] who had gone before me. I asked especially to be sustained should I be called to pass through the dark waters alone.

It was no idle prayer, and the response came swiftly. All anxieties and cares slipped away like a worn-out garment, and Christ's peace enfolded me. I was content to wait on God's time to see my loved ones, and told myself that if I did not see them again on earth, we would be reunited in heaven.

In spite of my agonized suffering, I was at peace, and felt that I had truly found the refuge of the "everlasting arms"[4]; I rested in them, as a tired child rests on its mother's breast.

———————⌒⌒———————

One dark, cold, and stormy morning, after a day and night of intense suffering, I seemed to be standing by the bed, in front of the stained-glass window. Someone was standing by me, and when I looked up I saw it was my husband's favorite brother, who had gone to heaven many years before.

"Frank!" I cried out joyously. "How good of you to come!"

"It gives me great joy to do so. Will you come with me now?" he asked, leading me to the window.

I turned my head and looked back into the room that I somehow felt I was about to leave forever. It was in its usual good order: a cheery, pretty room. My caregiver sat by the stove, reading a newspaper. On the bed, facing the window, lay a pale, still form, with the shadow of a smile on her face.

I went with Frank, passing through the window, out onto the porch, and then, in some unaccountable way, down to the street. There I paused and told him, "I cannot leave Will and our son."

---

3   Hebrews 1:14.
4   Deuteronomy 33:27.

"They are hundreds of miles away," he answered.

"Yes, I know, but they will be here. Oh, Frank! They will need me—let me stay!"

"Would it not be better if I brought you back a little later—after they arrive?" he asked, with a kind smile.

"Would you?" I asked.

"Certainly. But for now, you are worn out, and a little rest will renew your strength."

I agreed, and we started slowly up the street. He tried to interest me in the things around us as we walked. But I was still worrying about my family, and several times I stopped to look back the way we had come. He always waited patiently until I was ready.

At last my hesitation became so great that he said pleasantly, "You are so weak I think I had better carry you." Without waiting for a reply, he lifted me in his arms like a little child; and I yielded, resting my head on his shoulder, my arm about his neck. I felt so safe, so content, to be in his care after the long, lonely struggle, to have someone assume the responsibility of caring tenderly for me.

He walked on with firm, swift steps, and I must have slept.

The next thing I knew, I was sitting in a sheltered nook of flowering shrubs. I sat on the softest and most beautiful grass, thickly surrounded by fragrant flowers, many of them the ones I knew and loved on earth. I remember noticing heliotrope, violets, lily of the valley, and mignonette, and many others unfamiliar to me. Even in that first moment I observed that every plant and flower was perfect in its way.

And what a scene it was before me! Far beyond the limit of my vision stretched a wonderful expanse of perfect grass and flowers; and out of it grew equally wonderful trees, whose drooping branches were laden with exquisite blossoms and fruit of many kinds. I found myself thinking of St. John's vision on the Isle of Patmos and the "tree of life" that grew in the midst of the garden, "bearing twelve crops of fruit, . . . [and] the leaves were used for medicine to heal the nations."[5] Happy groups of little children laughed and played beneath the trees, running back and forth joyfully and catching in their hands bright-winged birds that flitted in and out among them, as though sharing in their play. All through the grounds, older people were walking: in groups, by twos, or alone, but all with an obvious air of peacefulness and happiness. They all were clothed in spotless white, though many wore or carried in their hands clusters of bright flowers. Looking at their happy faces and spotless robes, I thought, *They have washed their robes in the blood of the Lamb and made them white.*[6]

Wherever I looked I saw, half hidden by the trees, elegant and beautiful houses of strangely attractive architecture. Sparkling fountains dotted the landscape, and close to my nook a tranquil river flowed, with crystal-clear water. The paths that ran in many directions through the grounds appeared to be of pearl, spotless and pure, bordered on either side by narrow streams of clear, shining water, running over stones of gold. There was no shadow of dust anywhere, no taint of decay on fruit or flower; everything was perfect and pure. The grass and flowers appeared freshly washed by summer showers, and not a single blade was any color but the brightest green. The air was soft and balmy, but invigorating; and instead of sunlight there was a golden glow everywhere, something like a southern sunset in midsummer.

I gasped in delight, and heard Frank, who was standing beside me, say softly, "Well?" Looking up, I discovered that he was watching me

---

5 Revelation 22:2.
6 Revelation 7:14.

with keen enjoyment. In my surprise and delight, I had completely forgotten his presence.

Recalled to myself by his question, I faltered, "Oh, Frank, I—" and such an overpowering sense of God's goodness and my own unworthiness swept over me that I dropped my face into my hands and burst into uncontrollable sobs.

"Ah!" he said, in a tone of self-reproach, "I am inconsiderate." And lifting me gently to my feet, he said, "Come, I want to show you the river."

When we reached the brink of the river, only a few steps away, I found that the lovely meadow extended right to the water's edge, and in some places I saw the meadow flowers were even blooming down in the depths, among the many-colored pebbles with which the entire riverbed was lined.

"I want you to see these beautiful stones." Frank stepped into the water, urging me to follow.

I drew back. "It will be cold."

"Not in the least," he assured me. "Come."

"Dressed like this?" I said, glancing down at my lovely robe, which I found, to my great joy, was similar to those worn by the dwellers in this happy place.

"Just as you are," he said, with a reassuring smile.

I stepped into the gently flowing river, and to my great surprise found the water, in both temperature and density, almost identical with the air.

The stream grew deeper as we passed on, until I felt the soft, sweet ripples playing about my throat. When I stopped, my brother said, "A little farther still."

"It will go over my head!" I protested.

"Well, and what then?"

"I cannot breathe under the water—I will suffocate."

An amused twinkle came into his eyes, though he said soberly enough, "Those things don't happen here."

Realizing the absurdity of my position, I said with a laugh, "All right; come on," and plunged headlong into the bright water, which soon bubbled and rippled several feet above my head. I found I could not only breathe, but also laugh and talk, see and hear, as naturally under the water as above it. Like a joy-filled child on a new adventure, I sat down in the midst of the many-colored pebbles, and filled my hands with them. Frank lay down on them, as he would have done on the green meadow, and laughed and talked joyously with me.

"Do this," he said, rubbing his hands over his face, and running his fingers through his dark hair. I did, and the sensation was delightful. I threw back my loose sleeves and rubbed my arms, then my throat, and again thrust my fingers through my long, loose hair, thinking what a tangle it would be in when I left the water.

When we at last rose to return to land, I wondered what we would do for towels, and whether the lovely robe was entirely ruined. But as we neared the shore and my head once more emerged from the water, the moment the air struck my face and hair I realized that I would need no towel or brush. My skin, my hair, and my beautiful garments were as soft and dry as before the water touched them. My robe was made of material unlike anything I had ever seen. It was soft and light and shone with a faint luster, reminding me more of silk than anything else, only infinitely more beautiful. It fell about me in soft, graceful folds, which the water seemed to have rendered even more lustrous than before.

"What marvelous water! What wonderful air!" I said to my brother, as we stepped again onto the flowery meadow. "Are all the rivers here like this one?"

"Not just the same, but similar," he replied.

We walked on a few steps, and then I turned and looked back at the shining river. "Frank, what has that water done for me?" I asked. "I feel as though I could fly."

He looked at me with earnest, tender eyes, as he answered gently, "It has washed away the last of the earth life, and fitted you for the new life you have begun."

"It is divine!" I whispered.

"Yes, it is Divine," he said.

CHAPTER 2

We walked on for some distance in silence, my heart wrestling with thoughts of this strange new life, my eyes drinking in fresh beauty at every step. The houses we passed amazed me. They were built of the finest marbles, encircled by broad verandas, their roofs or domes supported by pillars. Winding steps led down to the pearl and golden walks. The style of the architecture was unlike anything I had ever seen, and the flowers and vines that grew luxuriantly everywhere surpassed in beauty even my most imaginative dreams. Happy faces looked out from these columned walls, and happy voices rang upon the clear air.

"Frank, where are we going?" I finally asked.

"Home, little sister."

"Home? We have a home here? Is it anything like these?" I felt a wild desire to cry out for joy.

"Come and see," was his only answer, as he turned into a side path leading toward an exquisitely beautiful house with columns of very light gray marble that shone invitingly through the green of the overhanging trees. Before I could join him, I heard a well-remembered voice close beside me.

"I just had to be the first to welcome you!" Looking around, I saw my dearly beloved friend, Mrs. Wickham.

"Oh!" I cried, as we met in a warm embrace.

"Please forgive me, Col. Sprague," she said a moment later, extending her hand to my brother-in-law. "It seems rude to come so early, but I heard that she was coming, and I could not wait. Now that I have seen her face, and heard her dear voice, I will be patient till I can have her for a long, long talk."

"You must come in and visit with her now," he invited.

"Please stay!" I urged.

"No, dear friends, not now. You know, my little Blossom,"—she used her old pet name for me—"we have all eternity before us! But you will bring her to me soon, Col. Sprague?"

"Just as soon as I may," he replied, with an expressive look into her eyes.

"Yes, I understand," she said softly, with a sympathetic glance at me. Then, with a warm handclasp, she urged, "Come very soon," and left us.

"What a joy to meet her again!" I said.

"Her home is not far away; you can see her often. She is indeed a lovely woman. Now, come, I want to welcome you to our home." He took my hand and led me up the low steps onto the broad veranda, with its beautiful inlaid floor of rare and costly marble. Between its massive columns, vines covered with rich, glossy leaves intermingled with colorful, fragrant flowers hung in heavy festoons. We paused a moment here, so I could see the charming view presented on every side.

"Heavenly!" I said.

"It is heavenly," he agreed. "It could not be anything else."

I smiled my acknowledgment of this truth—my heart was too full for words.

"The entire house, below and above, is surrounded by these broad verandas. But come inside now."

He led me through a doorway between the marble columns, into a large reception hall, with an inlaid floor, mullioned window, and broad, low stairway at the far end.

Before I could speak, Frank turned to me, and, taking both my hands, said: "Welcome, a thousand welcomes, dearest sister, to your heavenly home!"

"Is this beautiful place really going to be my home?" I was overcome with emotion.

"Yes, dear," he replied. "I built it for you and my brother, and I assure you it has been a labor of love."

"It is your home, and I am to stay with you?" I asked, a little confused.

"No, it is *your* home, and I am to stay with you until my brother comes."

He smiled, and continued, "We will enjoy the present, and we never will be far apart again. But come, I am eager to show you everything."

Turning to the left, he led me through the marble columns that seemed to substitute for doorways, into a large, oblong room. The walls and floor of the room were still of that exquisite light-gray marble, polished to the greatest luster; but walls and floors were covered with long-stemmed roses of every variety and color, from the deepest crimson to the most delicate shades of pink and yellow.

"Come inside," he invited.

"I don't want to crush those perfect flowers," I protested.

"Well, then, suppose we gather some of them."

I stooped to take a rose from the floor close to my feet, but I found it was imbedded in the marble. I tried another with the same result, then turned ask, "What does it mean? Do you mean to tell me that none of these are natural flowers?"

He nodded his head with a pleased smile, then said: "This room has a history. Come in and sit with me here on this window seat, where you can see the whole room, and let me tell you about it." I sat, and he continued.

"One day as I was busily working on the house, a group of young people, came to the door, and asked if they might enter. I invited them in, and one of them asked if this house really was for Mr. and Mrs. Sprague. "'It is,' I answered.

"'We used to know and love them. They are our friends, and the friends of our parents, and we want to know if we might do something to help you make it beautiful.'

"'Indeed you may,' I said, touched by the request. 'What can you do?'

"We were here at the time, and looking about, one of them asked, 'May we beautify this room?'

"'Certainly,' I said, wondering what they would try to do.

"At once the girls, who all carried immense bunches of roses in their hands, began to throw the flowers over the floor and against the walls. Wherever they struck the walls, they remained, as though in some way permanently attached. When the roses had all been scattered, the room looked just as it does now, only the flowers really were fresh-gathered roses. Then each of the boys produced a small case of delicate tools, and in a moment they all, boys and girls, were busy at work on the marble floor. How they did it I do not know—it is one of the celestial arts, taught to those of highly artistic tastes—but they embedded each living flower in the marble, just where and as it had fallen, and preserved it as you see before you.

"They came back several times before the work was completed, for the flowers do not wither or fade here, but were always fresh and perfect. I never before saw such a merry, happy group of young people. They laughed and chatted and sang as they worked; and I could not help wishing more than once that the grieving friends they left behind might look in on this happy group, and see how little cause there was to mourn.

"At last, when it was complete, they called me to see their work, and I praised not only the beauty of the work but also their skill in doing it. Then, saying they would be sure to return when either of you came, they went away together, to make something beautiful in another place, I imagine."

Happy tears falling, for I was greatly touched, I asked, "Who were these lovely people, Frank? Do you know them?"

"Of course, I know them now; but they were all strangers to me that first morning, except Lulu Sprague."

"Who are they?"

"The girls were Mary Green, Mary Bates, Mary Chalmers, Lulu Sprague, and Mae Camden. Carroll Ashland, and Stanley and David Chalmers were the boys."

"Precious children!" I said. "I never would have imagined that my love for them would bring me this added happiness here! How little we know of the links binding the two worlds!"

"Ah, yes!" he agreed. "That is just it: how little we know! If only we could realize while we are still on earth that every day there we are building for eternity, how different in many ways our lives would be! We cannot be selfish and unloving in one life, and generous and loving in the next; the two lives are too closely blended—one a continuation of the other.

"But come now to the library." Rising, we crossed the rose room, which from now on would always make me think of the children who lovingly created it for us, and entered the library.

The library was a wonderful place, its walls lined from ceiling to floor with rare and costly books. A large stained-glass window opened to the front veranda, and there were two large bow windows, not far apart, in the back wall of the room. A semicircular row of shelves, supported by very delicate, gray marble pillars about six feet high, extended into the spacious main room. The concave side of the shelves was toward the entrance of the room; and close to it, near a window, stood a beautiful writing desk, with everything ready for use; on the desk was a golden bowl filled with scarlet carnations, of whose spicy odor I had been dimly conscious for some time.

"My brother's desk," said Frank.

"And his favorite flowers," I added.

"Yes, of course. Here we never forget the tastes and preferences of those we love."

I did not notice all these details right away; rather, they unfolded to me gradually as we lingered, talking together. My first sensation upon entering the room was genuine surprise at the sight of the books, and my first words were: "Why do we have books in heaven?"

"Why not?" asked my brother-in-law. "What strange ideas we mortals have of the pleasures and duties of the heavenly life! We seem to think that death of the body means an entire change to the soul; but that is not the case, by any means. What would be the use of a long life, given to the pursuit of worthy and legitimate knowledge, if at death it all counts as nothing, and we begin this life on a wholly different line of thought and study? No use at all! I wish that mortals could understand, as I said before, that we are building for eternity during our earthly life! The more earnestly we follow the studies and duties given to us in our life of earthly preparation, the better fitted we shall be to carry them forward to completion and perfection here."

"But the books—who writes them? Are any of them books we knew and loved below?"

"Undoubtedly, many of them are; all, indeed, that in any way helped to elevate the human mind or immortal soul. Many of the rarest minds in the earth life, when they enter here, gain such elevated and extended views of the subjects they have studied in their earthly lives that they write out for the benefit of those less gifted, the higher, stronger views they have themselves acquired; in this way, they remain leaders and teachers here, as they were in the world.

Do we think that a godly evangelist like Henry Drummond[7], who is in our ranks and whose *Changed Life* and *Pax Vobiscum* uplifted so many lives while on earth, should lay his pen aside when now his clear brain and great heart have solved the mystery of the higher knowledge? Not so. As he learns his lessons well on this side of the veil, he will write them out for the benefit of others who follow. There must always be leaders, in this divine life just as in the former life—leaders and teachers in many varied areas. But all this knowledge will come to you easily and naturally as you grow into the new life."

---

7   Henry Drummond (1851–1897) was a Scottish evangelist, writer and lecturer. He wrote many books including the bestselling *The Greatest Thing in the World*. For more information see http://henrydrummond.wwwhubs.com.

CHAPTER 3

After a short rest in the library, Frank took me through all the remaining rooms of the house, each perfect and beautiful in its way. I remember them all as clearly as photographs, but will describe only one other here.

Drawing aside gauzy gray draperies lined with the most delicate shade of amber, which hung in the columned doorway of a lovely room on the second floor of the house, Frank said, "This is your own special place for rest and study."

The entire second story of the house, instead of being done in gray marble indoors, like the first floor, was finished with inlaid woods of fine, satiny texture. The room we now entered was exquisite: oblong in shape, with a large bowed window at one end, similar to those in the library. Tucked into one side of the curved window was a writing desk of solid ivory, with silver appointments; opposite it was a well-filled bookcase of the same material. I later found many of my favorite authors among the books. Rich rugs, silver-gray in color, lay scattered over the floor, and all the hangings in the room were of the same delicate hue and texture as those at the entrance. The framework of the furniture was of ivory; chairs, ottomans, and a dainty couch were upholstered in silver-gray cloth, with the finish of finest satin. A large silver bowl on the table near the front window was filled with pink and yellow roses, whose fragrance filled the air; and several graceful vases also were filled with roses. The room was beautiful beyond description; but I saw it many times before I was able to fully appreciate its perfect completeness.

A life-size portrait of Christ, hung on the wall just opposite the couch, was the only picture in the room. It was not an artist's conception of the human Christ, bowed under the weight of the sins of the world, or of the thorn-crowned head of the crucified Savior of mankind, but the likeness of the living Master, Christ the victorious, Christ the crowned. The wonderful eyes looked directly and tenderly into your own, and His lips seemed to pronounce the benediction of peace. The indescribable beauty of His face seemed to fill the room with a holy light, and I fell to my knees and pressed my lips to the sandaled feet portrayed so lifelike on the canvas, while my heart cried, "Master, beloved Lord and Savior!" It was a long while before I could fix my attention on anything else; my whole being was full of adoration and thanksgiving for the great love that had guided me into this haven of rest, this wonderful home of peace and joy.

After some time spent in this delightful place, we passed through the open window onto the marble terrace. A stairway of artistically finished marble wound gracefully down from this terrace to the lawn beneath the trees. The fruit-laden branches of the trees hung within easy reach from the terrace, and I noticed seven varieties as I stood there that morning. One kind resembled our fine Bartlett pear, only much larger, and infinitely more delicious to the taste, as I soon learned. Another variety hung in clusters, its smaller fruit also pear-shaped, and of a consistency and flavor similar to the finest ice cream. A third, shaped something like a banana, they called bread-fruit; it was not unlike our dainty finger rolls to the taste. It seemed to me at the time, and proved to be true, that in variety and excellence, food for the most elegant gourmet meal was provided here without labor or care. Frank gathered some of the different varieties for me to try; they were delicious and refreshing. When the rich juice from a pearl-like fruit (whose distinctive name I have forgotten, if I ever knew it) dripped all over my hands and the front of my dress, I cried, "Oh no! I have ruined my dress!"

Frank laughed as he said, "Show me the stains."

To my amazement, I could not find a single spot.

"Look at your hands," he said. I found them clean and fresh, as though just washed.

"What does it mean? My hands were covered with fruit juice."

"Simply," he answered, "that no impurity can remain for an instant in this air. Nothing decays, nothing tarnishes, or in any way disfigures or mars the universal purity and beauty of the place. As the fruit ripens and falls, all that is not immediately gathered evaporates at once, not even the seed remaining."

"'Nothing impure will ever enter it, '" I quoted.[8]

"Yes," he answered, "it is so."

We descended the steps and again entered the rose room. As I stood once more admiring the inlaid flowers, Frank asked, "Of all the friends you have in heaven, whom do you most wish to see?"

"My father and mother," I answered quickly.

He smiled so significantly that I quickly turned, and there, coming up the long room to meet me, I saw my dear father and mother, and my youngest sister with them. With a cry of joy, I flew into my father's outstretched arms, and heard, with a thrill of joy, his familiar, "My precious daughter!"

"At last!" I cried, clinging to him. "I'm finally with you again!"

8   Revelation 21:27 NIV.

"At last!" he echoed, with a joyful sigh. Then he handed me over to my dear mother, and we were soon clasped in each other's embrace.

"Mother!" "My dear, dear child!" We cried out simultaneously; and my sister, enfolding us both in her arms, exclaimed with a happy laugh, "I can't wait! I will not be left out!" Disengaging one arm, I pulled her into a group hug.

Oh, what a reunion—I had no earthly dream that even heaven could hold such joy!

After a time Frank, who had shared our joy, said, "Now I can safely leave you for a few hours to this family reunion; I have other work to attend to."

"Yes," my father agreed, "you go ahead. We are delighted to take charge of our dear child."

"Then, good-bye for a little while," Frank said, adding, "Do not forget that rest is not only one of the pleasures, but one of the duties of heaven—especially for one so new here."

"We will see that she remembers that," my father assured him.

CHAPTER 4

Soon after Frank left us, my mother, grasping my hand, said, "Come, I am eager to have you in our own home."

We all went out the back door, walked a few hundred yards across the soft turf, and entered a lovely house, somewhat similar to the one Frank had built for me and my husband, but still unique in many details. It was built of a darker marble than ours. Every room spoke of modest refinement and cultivated taste, and it had an immediate feeling of home about it. My father's study was on the second floor, and the first thing I noticed there was that lush branches and flowers of an old-fashioned cabbage rose covered the window by his desk.

"Ah!" I cried, "When I look at that window, I can almost imagine myself in your old study at home."

"It really is a reminder, isn't it?" he said, laughing happily. "Sometimes I almost think it is the same dear old bush, transplanted here."

"Is it still your favorite flower?" I asked.

He nodded and said, smiling, "I see you still remember your childhood days." He patted my cheek as I picked a rose and fastened it to his robe.

"It seems to me this ought to be your home too; it is our father's home," my sister said wistfully.

"No," my father interrupted. "Col. Sprague is her guardian and instructor here. It is a wise arrangement. He is in every way the most suitable instructor she could possibly have. Our Father is never wrong."

"Frank really is a special person," I observed.

"Special indeed; and he stands very near to the Master. Few have a clearer knowledge of the divine will than Frank, so there are few who are better suited to be instructors. But I also have duties that call me away for a time. What a blessing it is to know there can never again be long separations! You will have two homes now, dear child—your own and ours."

"Yes!" I said. "I suspect I will be here almost as much as there."

At this moment a swift messenger approached my father and spoke a few low words.

"Yes, I will go at once," he replied, and departed with the angelic guide.

"What are my father's duties here?" I asked my mother.

"He is usually called to assist those who enter this life with little preparation—what we called on earth death-bed conversion. You know what wonderful success he always had in winning souls to Christ; and these poor spirits need to be taught from the very beginning. They enter the spirit life in its lowest level, and it is your father's pleasant duty to guide them upward step by step. He is devoted to his work and greatly beloved by those he helps. I am often able to work with him, and that is such a pleasure to me! And do you know"—she ended with a joyful smile—"I forget nothing now!"

For several years before her death, my mother was burdened by a failing memory, and I could understand her present delight.

"How wonderful!" I hugged her gently. "You mean you are able to work together again like you did in the early years of your married life?"

"Precisely!" She smiled again.

A little later my sister drew me aside and whispered, "Tell me about my precious son. I often see him, but we are not permitted to know as much about the earthly life as we once believed we should. The Father's tender wisdom measures out to us the knowledge He deems best, and we are content to wait His time for more. Please tell me: Is he coming to me someday? Will I hold him in my arms again?"

"Yes, I am sure you will. His memories of you are very precious to him."

Then I told her all I could recall of the son with whom she had parted while he was only a child—now grown into an honored and loved man, with his own home and blessed with a wife and son of his own.

"Then I can wait," she said, "if he is sure to come to me at last, when his earthly work is done, and bring his wife and son. I will love them too!"

At this moment I felt myself encircled by tender arms, and a hand was gently laid on my eyes.

"Guess who," someone whispered softly.

"Oh, I know your voice and your touch—Nell!" I cried, and, turning quickly, threw my arms about the neck of my only brother.

He held me close for a moment; then, in the playful way I remembered so well, lifted me off my feet in his strong arms, saying, "She has not grown an inch and is not, I believe, a day older than when we last parted! Is she, Jo?" he said, turning to our sister.

"So it seems," she replied, "but I thought she would never get here."

"Trust her for that!" he said. "But come, now—they have had you long enough for the first visit; the rest of us want you for a while. Come with us, Jodie. Mother, may I have them both for a little while? Or will you come too?" he asked, turning to our mother with a caress.

"I can't go; I must be here when your father returns. Take your sisters;

it is a blessed sight to see you all again together."

"Come then," he said and, hand in hand, we went out together.

"Halt!" he suddenly called, in his military fashion, after a short walk. We stopped abruptly in front of a beautiful, dainty house built of the finest polished woods.

"How lovely!" I exclaimed.

With a charming little bow, he said, "The home of your humble servant. Enter."

I paused a moment on the wide porch to examine a vine that wreathed around its graceful columns, and my brother said laughingly to our sister:

"She is the same old Sis! We will not get much good out of her until she has learned the name of every flower, vine, and plant in heaven."

"Yes, you will," I replied, "but I mean to take advantage of every opportunity; I have so much to learn."

"And so you should, dear," he answered gently. "But do come in now." Stepping inside a lovely entry hall, out of which spacious rooms opened from every side, he called softly, "Alma!" At once, a fair woman approached us from one of the rooms.

"It does not seem possible!" I said. "You were just a child when I last saw you."

"She is still her father's girl," said my brother, with a fond look. "She and Carrie, whom you never saw, make a blessed home for me. Where is your sister, daughter?"

"She's at the great music hall. She has a very rich voice that she is cultivating," Alma said, turning to me. "We were going to find our aunt when she returned," she added to her father.

"Well, we are here now," said my brother, "so let's show her around."

Their home was lovely, perfect and charming in every detail. When we came out onto a side veranda, I saw that we were so near an adjoining house we could easily step from one veranda to the other.

"There!" said my brother, easily lifting me over the intervening space. "There is someone here you will want to see." Before I could question him, he led me through the columned doorway, saying, "People in heaven are never unavailable to their friends."

The house we entered was almost identical to my brother Nell's, and as we entered, three persons came eagerly forward to greet me.

"Dear Aunt Gray!" I cried. "And Mary—my dear Martin! What a joy to see you all again!"

"And in this place," said my aunt reverently.

"Yes," I answered in like tone.

It was my father's sister, always a favorite aunt, with her son and his wife. We talked excitedly and clung to one another, asking and answering questions all at the same time.

"Pallas is also here, and Will, but they have gone with Carrie to the music hall," Martin told me.

"Martin, can you sing here?" I asked. He was always trying to sing on earth, but could not carry a tune.

"A little," he answered, with his old genial laugh and a shrug. "We can do almost anything here that we really try to do."

"You should hear him now, cousin, when he tries to sing," said his wife, with a little touch of pride in her voice. "You would not know it was Martin. But isn't it nice to have Dr. Nell so near us? We are almost one household, you know. We all felt that we must be together."

"It is indeed," I answered, "although you no longer need him in his professional capacity."

"No, thanks to the Father, we don't; but we need him just as much in many other ways."

"I rather think I am the one who should be grateful," said my brother. "But, sister, I promised Frank that you would go to your own room for a while; he thought it would be wise for you to have some time alone.

Shall we go now?"

"I am ready," I answered, "even though these delightful reunions leave me with no desire for rest."

"How blessed we are," said my aunt, "that there is no limit here to our mutual enjoyment! We have nothing to dread, nothing to fear. We know when we part that we will meet again. We shall see each other often, my child."

Then my brother walked with me to my own home, and, with a loving embrace, left me at the door of my room.

Once alone, I lay down on my couch to think over the events of this wonderful day; but, looking upward at the divine face above me, I forgot all else. Christ's peace enfolded me like a soft cloak, and I became "as one whom his mother comforts."[9]

While I lay in this blissful rest, Frank returned and, without waking me, carried me in his strong arms back to earth.

I did not know, when Frank left me with my parents, what mission he was going on. My father knew Frank had gone to accompany his brother—my dear husband—on his sad journey to his dead wife, to comfort and sustain and strengthen him in those first lonely hours of sorrow. For wise reasons, Frank and my parents deemed it best for me not to return to earth immediately with Frank. They felt I should continue my introduction to the blessings of the new life, rest and gain strength for the difficult task ahead.

9 Isaiah 66:13 (NKJV)

CHAPTER 5

When I woke in the gray light of earth's morning, I was standing on the doorstep of the house in Kentville that my brother-in-law and I had left together some thirty-six hours before, according to earth time. I shuddered a little with a strange chill when I saw where we were, and turned quickly to Frank, who stood beside me. He put his arm around me, and said, with a reassuring smile:

"For their sakes be brave and strong, and try to make them understand how you have been changed."

I did not answer, though his words encouraged me, and together we entered the house. Everything was very quiet—it seemed no one was awake yet. My brother opened a door immediately to the right of the entrance, and motioned me to enter. I did, and he closed it behind me, remaining outside.

A coffin stood in the center of the room. I was relieved to see that the pall covering it was not black, but a soft shade of gray. Someone was kneeling beside it, and as I approached I saw it was my dear son. He knelt there with his face buried in his hand and one arm thrown across the casket, as though he was sharing a last embrace. I saw that the form within the casket lay as though peacefully sleeping, and was dressed in silver gray, with soft white folds about the neck and breast. I was grateful that they had remembered my wishes so well.

I put my arms around the neck of my darling son, and drew his head gently against my breast, resting my cheek on his bowed head. Then I whispered, "Dearest, I am here beside you—living, breathing, strong and well. Will you not turn to me, instead of to that lifeless form in the casket? It is only the worn-out shell—I am your living mother."

He lifted his head as though listening; then, laying his hand tenderly against the white face in the casket, he whispered, "Poor, dear little mother!" and dropped his face into both hands, his body shaking with convulsive sobs.

As I tried to comfort him, the door opened and his lovely young wife entered. I turned to meet her as she came slowly toward us. Midway in the room we met, and, taking her hands in mine, I whispered, "Comfort him, darling girl, as only you can; he needs human love."

She hesitated a moment, looking directly into my eyes, then moved on and knelt beside her husband, laying her face against his shoulder. I saw him reach out and draw her closely to him, then I left the room, feeling comforted that they were together.

Outside the door I paused for a moment, then slowly ascended the stairs and entered the once-familiar sickroom. The door stood ajar and everything remained as it was when I left it, except that no still form lay upon the white bed. As I expected, I found my precious husband in this room. He sat near the bay window, his arm resting on the table, and his eyes turned to the floor. My best friend sat near him, trying to comfort him. When I entered, Frank rose from a chair close beside them and left, with a sympathetic look at me. I went at once to my dear husband, put my arms around him, and whispered:

"Darling, I am here!"

He stirred restlessly without changing his position.

Virginia said, as though continuing a conversation, "I am sure she would say you left nothing undone that could possibly be done for her."

"She is right," I whispered.

"I left her alone at the end," he moaned.

"Yes, dear, but who could know it was the end? She went so suddenly. What can I say to comfort you? Oh, Will, please come home with us! She would want you to, I am sure."

He shook his head sadly, tears in his eyes, as he said, "I have to work. I need to go back in a very few days."

She said no more, and he leaned back wearily. I crept closer to him and suddenly his arms seemed to close around me. I whispered, "There, dear, do you not see that I am really with you?"

He was very still, and the room was quiet except for the ticking of my little clock still standing on the dresser. Soon I could tell by his regular breathing that he had found a short respite from his sorrow. I slipped gently from his arms and went to my friend, kneeling beside her, and folding my arms about her.

"Virginia, Virginia! You know I am not dead! Why do you grieve?"

She looked over at the worn face of the man beside her, then dropped her face into her hands, whispering, as though she had heard me:

"Oh, Rebecca darling, how could you leave him?"

"I am here, dearest! Please know that I am here!"

She paid no attention to me.

A few minutes later a stranger entered the room, and in a low voice said something about it being "nearly time for the train," and brought my husband his hat. He rose and gave his arm to Virginia; our son and his wife met them at the door, and they started to descend the stairs. Just then my husband paused and cast one sorrowful glance around the room, his face white with pain. Our dear daughter-in-law stepped quickly to him, and, placing both arms about his neck, drew his face down to hers. ("God bless her in all things!" I softly prayed.) They stood this way for only a moment, then he stifled his emotion, and they all went downstairs into the room I had first entered.

I stayed very close to my husband, and never left his side for a single moment through all the solemn funeral service, the sad journey to our old home, the last rites at the graveside, the visiting with friends afterward, and his eventual return to the weary routine of his work. How thankful I was that I had been permitted to taste, during that one wonderful day in heaven, the joys of eternal life! How else could I ever have passed calmly through those difficult events, and witnessed the sorrow of those so dear to me? I recognize the wisdom and mercy of the Father in having planned it this way.

I soon found that my husband was right: work was his great refuge. During the day the routine kept mind and hands busy, leaving his heart little opportunity to indulge its sorrow. Night was his trying time. Kind friends stayed with him till bedtime; after that he was alone. He would turn and toss restlessly on his pillow, and often get up to go into the adjoining room that had been mine, where he would stare at the vacant bed with tearful eyes. It took all my powers to comfort and quiet him even a little. After a time, Frank and I arranged to spend alternate nights with him, so he would never be left alone, and we went with him on his journeys. We found to our great joy that our influence over him grew stronger, and we were able to guide and help him in many ways.

One night, many months after my death, I was silently watching beside him while he slept, when I became aware that danger threatened him. He was sleeping very peacefully, and I knew his dreams were happy ones by the smile on his face. I went into the hall of the hotel where he was staying, and found it dense with smoke. Hurrying back to him, I called out, and tried to shake him, but he slept on. Finally, I yelled close to his ear with all my strength, "Will!"

Instantly he started up and said, "Yes, dear, I am coming!" just as he used to do when I called out for him at night. Then in a moment he sank back upon his pillow with a sigh, murmuring, "What a vivid dream! I never heard her voice more distinctly when she was alive."

"Will!" I called again, pulling him by the hand with all my strength, "Get up! Your life is in danger!"

In an instant he was out of bed, on his feet, and hurriedly throwing on his clothes. "I don't know why I am doing this," he muttered to himself. "I only know that I must! That was certainly her voice I heard."

"Hurry! Hurry!" I urged.

He opened the door and met not only the smoke, but also a wall of flame.

"Do not try the stairway—come this way!" I guided him through a narrow entrance to a second hall beyond, and down a second flight of stairs, filled with smoke, but as yet no flame. There was another flight still below these, then we were outside in the open air, where he staggered, faint and exhausted, onto the sidewalk, and was quickly helped by friends to a safe place.

"I don't know what woke me," he told a friend later. "I dreamed I heard my wife calling me, and before I knew it I was getting dressed."

"You did hear her, I have no doubt," his friend replied. "Are they not all 'servants—spirits sent to care for people who will inherit salvation'[10]? What more loving service could she do than to save the life of one so dear to her, whose work on earth was not yet done? Yes, you did hear her call you in time to escape. Thank God for such servants!"

"Yes, that must be true," he answered, with a happy look. "Thank God indeed."

---

10   Hebrews 1:14.

After this he yielded much more readily to our influence, and so began to enjoy, while still on earth, the reunion that so surely awaited us in heaven. I also went often to our son's home, but there was so much to make them happy that they did not need me as much as my husband did. Sometimes when he was exhausted, especially if his wife was away from home, I found that I could quiet my dear son, and lead his tired mind to restful thoughts; but with youth and strength and love to support him, the time had not yet come when my care was essential to him.

CHAPTER 6

The first time I returned to my heavenly home after a long delay on earth, as I approached the entrance with Frank, we saw a tall young man standing near the open gate, looking wistfully toward the way we came. As we drew near, he asked in a pleading voice, "Is my mother coming?"

With a closer look I recognized him, and I exclaimed with joy, reaching out to him, "My dear Carroll!"

He smiled a bright welcome as he extended his hands, but said wistfully, "I so hoped my mother would return with you, aunt, when you came back. Did you see her?"

"Only once, for a brief moment. She is very happy and carries her years well. She will come to you before long now, and when she does, you know it will be forever."

"Yes, I know." His face brightened. "I will be patient. But," he added confidentially, "I so want her to see the lovely home I am building for her. Will you come and see it?"

"Of course I will, gladly."

"Now?"

"Yes, if I may." I looked to Frank for his approval. He nodded his head pleasantly as he said, "That's right, Carroll. Have her help you in every way you can. I will leave you two together, and you will bring her to me later, okay?"

"Certainly," my nephew agreed, and we went away happily together.

"Where is this wonderful house, Carroll?"

"Not very far beyond Mrs. Wickham's."

We soon reached it, and I was truly charmed by it in every way. It was designed much like my brother Nell's home, and was also built of polished woods. It was only partly finished, but the craftsmanship was excellent. Although the work was uncompleted, I was struck by the fact that everything was perfect so far. There was no debris anywhere: no wood chips, no shavings, no dust. The wood seemed to have been perfectly prepared elsewhere—where, I have no idea—and brought clean to the building site. The pieces were made to fit together perfectly, like the parts of a great puzzle. It seemed to me that much skill and artistic taste would be required to properly place each one. This, my nephew—who even in his earthly life was quite a mechanical genius—seemed to have no difficulty in doing, and the house was steadily growing into beautiful symmetry. After showing me all over the house, he at last drew aside the hangings at the entrance to two rooms that were entirely finished, and beautifully furnished as well.

"I finished and furnished these rooms first, so that if mother arrived before the house was ready, she could occupy them at once. You know there is no construction noise here—no hammering, no unwelcome sounds."

I thought at once of the Temple of Jerusalem, and how Scripture explains that "the stones used in the construction of the Temple were finished at the quarry, so there was no sound of hammer, ax, or any other iron tool at the building site."[11]

---

11   1 Kings 6:7.

"It is very beautiful," I said enthusiastically. "It will give her great joy to know you did it for her. But what is this—a fireplace?" I paused in front of a lovely open chimney, where wood was piled ready to be lighted. "Is it ever cold enough here for fires?"

"It is never cold," he answered, "but the fire here never sends out unneeded warmth. We have its cheer and beauty and glow, without any of its discomforts. You remember my mother loves to sit by an open fire; so I have arranged this for her."

"It is charming! But surely you did not make the stained-glass windows too?"

"No, I have a friend who has been taught that art, and we exchange work. He helps me with the windows, and I in turn help him with his fine woodwork and inlaying. I am going to make a flower room for my mother similar to yours, only with lilies and violets, which will keep their fragrance always."

"How lovely! I want to thank you, dear Carroll, for your share in our flower room. It is the most exquisite work I ever saw; and it is doubly appreciated when I remember whose hands fashioned it."

"It was a labor of love for us all," he said simply.

"That is what enhances its beauty for me," I said. "But sit here beside me now, and tell me about yourself. Do you spend all your time at this delightful work?"

"Oh, no! Perhaps only what we would call on earth two or three hours daily. Much of my time is still spent with my grandfather. I don't know what I would have done without his help when I first arrived. I was so ignorant about this life, and came here so suddenly."

"Yes, dear boy, I know," I said sympathetically.

"He met me at the very entrance, and took me home at once, where he and Grandma did everything possible to instruct and help me. But I was—I still am—far below where I ought to be. I would go back to the earthly life for an entire year if only I could go to my old friends—or better yet, into every Sunday school in the world—and beg the girls and boys to try to understand and live by what they are taught there. I used to go to Sunday school, week after week; I sang the hymns, and read the lesson, and listened to all that was said; and I really enjoyed every moment of it. Sometimes I would feel a great longing for a better life, but there seemed to be no one to guide or help me to find it, and, most of the time, what I heard one Sunday was never once spoken about or even thought of till another Sunday came, so that the impression made on me was very fleeting. Why don't boys and girls talk more together about what they hear at Sunday school? We were all ready enough to talk about a show of any kind after it was over, but seldom of Sunday school, when we were just hanging out together socially. Why don't Sunday-school teachers take more interest in the daily lives of their students? Why is there so little really helpful talk in ordinary home life? Oh, I wish I could go back and tell them how important it is!"

His face beamed with enthusiasm as he talked, and I too wished it was possible for him to do as he desired. But I recalled that Jesus told His disciples, "They will not be convinced even if someone rises from the dead."[12]

"It's time now for me to go with my grandfather," he said, rising, "but we will walk together as far as your home; and you will let me see you often, won't you?"

"Gladly," I answered, as we set forth.

We talked of many things as we walked, and when we parted at my door I said, "I am soon going to learn how to weave draperies; then I can help you, when you are ready for them."

"That will make my work more delightful still," he replied, and he hurried off in the direction of my parents' home.

---

12   Luke 16:31 (NIV)

CHAPTER 7

As time passed, and I became more accustomed to the heavenly life, its loveliness unfolded to me like the slow opening of a rare flower. Delightful surprises met me at every turn. I would unexpectedly meet a dear friend, who had gone to heaven years ago. Or someone I had greatly admired on earth, but not approached for fear of unwelcome intrusion, would approach me, revealing a lovely soul full of kindness and a similar disposition to my own—and I would feel a pang of regret for not having known them on earth. Or yet again, some truth that I tried to understand on earth would be revealed to me with such clarity and strength that I would feel overwhelmed by its brilliance, and often would see in it even more evidence of the close ties between the earthly life and the divine.

Most wonderful of all to me was the occasional meeting with someone I had known on earth but thought I would never see in heaven who, with warm hugs and tearful eyes, would pour forth his earnest thanks for some helpful word, solemn warning, or even stern rebuke, that had turned him, unknown to me, from the paths of sin into the life everlasting. Oh, the joy I felt from such a revelation! And oh, the regret that my earthly life had not been filled with such work for eternity!

Every morning, when I woke from a blissful rest, my first impulse was to go to the river of life and plunge into its wonderful waters, so refreshing, invigorating, and inspiring. With a heart full of thanksgiving and my voice expressing joyful praise, morning after morning—sometimes with Frank, sometimes alone—I hurried there, always returning home filled with new life, hope, and purpose. I spent time each day listening to the entrancing revelations and instructions of my brother-in-law.

One morning, soon after I returned from my first visit to earth, I was on the way to the river, my voice joining in the wonderful anthem of praise that sounded all around, when I saw a lovely young girl approaching swiftly, with outstretched arms.

"Dear, dear Aunt Rebecca!" she called, as she drew near, "Do you not recognize me?"

"My little Mae!" I cried, gathering the dainty creature into my arms. "Where did you spring from so suddenly? Let me look at you!" I held her a moment at arm's length, but quickly drew her close again.

"You have grown very beautiful, child. You were always lovely; you are simply radiant now. Is it this divine life?"

"Yes," she said modestly and sweetly, "but most of all it is from being near the Savior so much."

"Of course, that is it! Being close to Him will make any person radiant and beautiful."

"He is so good to me, so generous, so tender! He seems to forget how little I have done to deserve His care."

"He knows you love Him, dear; that means everything to Him."

"Love Him! Oh, if simply loving Him deserves reward, I am sure I ought to have every wish of my heart granted, for I love Him a thousand times better than anything in earth or heaven. I would die for Him!"

Her sweet face grew even more radiant and beautiful as she talked, and I began to perceive the matchless power of Christ among the redeemed in heaven. This dear child was lovely in all the earthly ways. She was pure and good, as we count goodness on earth, but so occupied with earth's keenest enjoyments during her brief life—seemingly too absorbed in life's fun to think deeply of the things she nevertheless revered and honored in her heart. Now in heavenly life she counted the privilege of loving Christ, of being near Him, better than every other joy. And how that love refined and beautified her!

As a great earthly love shines through the face and elevates the whole character of the one who loves, even more so does divine love uplift and enhance the giver, until not only the face but the entire person radiates the glory of the One who fills the heart.

"Come with me to the river, Mae," I invited, after we had talked together for a while.

"Gladly," she said, "but have you ever been to the lake or the sea?"

"The lake or the sea?" I echoed. "No indeed. Are there a lake and sea here?"

"Certainly there are," said Mae, with a little pardonable pride that she should know more of the heavenly surroundings than I. "Shall we go to the lake today, and leave the sea for another day? Which would you prefer?"

"Let's go to the lake today."

So, turning in an entirely different direction from the path that led to the river, we walked on, still talking as we went. We had so much to ask each other, so much to recall, so much to look forward to with joy!

Once she turned to me and asked quickly, "When is my Uncle Will coming?"

My hand closed tightly over hers, and a sob almost rose in my throat, though I answered calmly, "That is in God's hands alone; we must not question His will."

"Yes, I know. His will is always right; but I so long to see my dear uncle again—and to long for it does not mean I am discontent."

She had grown so womanly—so wise for a child of tender years—since we parted, that it was a joy to talk with her. I told her about my sad errand to earth, and the sorrow of the dear ones I had left.

"Yes, yes, I know it all!" she whispered, with her soft arms about me. "But you will not have to wait long; they will come soon. It never seems long to wait for anything here. There is always so much to do, so many pleasant duties, so many joys—oh, I promise you, it will not be long!"

She continued to cheer and comfort me as we walked through the ever-varying and always-perfect landscape. At last she lifted her arm and, pointing with her rosy finger, cried, "Look! Isn't it divinely beautiful?"

I caught my breath, then stopped suddenly and covered my face with my hands to shield my eyes from the glorious scene. No wonder my brother had not yet brought me to this place; I was still barely strong enough spiritually to look at it. When I slowly lifted my head, Mae was standing like one entranced. The golden morning light touched her face and, mingling with the radiance from inside, almost transfigured her. Even she, a longtime inhabitant here, did not take its glory for granted.

"Look, darling auntie! It is God's will that you should see," she softly whispered, not once turning her eyes away from the scene before her. "He has allowed me to be the one to show you the glory of this place!"

I turned and looked, but like one only half awake. Before us spread a lake as smooth as glass, flooded with a golden light from the heavens that made it like a sea of molten gold. Blossom- and fruit-bearing trees grew down to the water's edge in many places, and far away, across its shining waters, rose the domes and spires of what seemed to be a mighty city. Many people rested on its flowery banks, and on the surface of the water floated magnificent boats filled with happy souls and propelled by an unseen power. Little children, as well as grown persons, were floating or swimming in the water; and as we looked a band of singing cherubs, floating high overhead, drifted across the lake, their baby voices carrying to us where we stood, in notes of joyful praise.

"Come," Mae said, grabbing my hand, "let's join them!"

"Glory and honor!" sang the child voices. "Dominion and power!" answered the voices of the vast multitude together, and I found that Mae and I were joining in their song. The cherub band floated on, and in the distance we caught the faint melody of their sweet voices, and the stronger cadence of the response from those below.

We stood on the shore of the lake; and my cheeks were wet with tears and my vision blurred with emotion. I felt weak as a newborn baby, but filled and overcome with rapture and unspeakable joy. Was I dreaming? Or was this really just another phase of the immortal life?

Mae slipped her arm about my neck and whispered, "Come. After all of this excitement it is good to rest."

I yielded passively to her coaxing and she led me into the water. We went down, down into its crystal depths, and when it seemed to me we must be hundreds of feet beneath the surface, Mae stretched her body out and motioned to me to do the same. Immediately we began to slowly rise. After a while I noticed that we no longer rose, but were floating calmly in mid current, still many feet beneath the surface. Wherever I looked, perfect rays of light surrounded me. I seemed to be resting in the heart of a prism, with vivid yet delicate coloring such as mortal eyes had never seen. Instead of seven colors of the spectrum, as we see them on earth, the colors blended in such a fine graduation of shades that the rays seemed almost infinite, or else they really were so; I could not decide which.

As I lay watching, the colors deepened and faded like the lights of the aurora borealis, and I could hear the sound of distant music. Although Mae and I no longer clung to one another, we did not drift apart, as one would naturally suppose we might, but lay within easy speaking distance, though few words were spoken by either of us; the silence seemed too sacred to be lightly broken. We lay within the water, as if we rested upon the softest couch. It required no effort whatever to keep ourselves afloat; the gentle undulation of the waves soothed and restored us.

When the far-off music caught my attention, I turned and looked at Mae. She smiled at me, but did not speak. I heard the words, "Glory and honor, dominion and power," and I knew it was still the cherub choir, although they must be many miles away by now. Then the soft tones of a bell—like a silver bell with silver tongue—fell on my ear, and as the last notes died away, I whispered, "Tell me, Mae."

"Yes, I will. The waters of this lake catch the light in a special way, as you have seen—a wiser head than mine will have to tell you why. The water also transmits musical sounds—but only musical sounds—for a great distance. The song was evidently from the distant shore of the lake."

"And the bell?"

"That is the bell in the city across the lake that calls some to certain commitments at this hour."

"There was never a sweeter call to duty," I said.

"Yes, its notes are beautiful. Listen!"

As we lay and listened, a sweet spell wrapped round me, and I slept as peacefully as a child on its mother's bosom. I woke with a strange sense of invigoration and strength. It was a totally different feeling to that experienced during a bath in the river, but I could not say how. Mae explained: "One takes away the last of the mortal life, and prepares us for the life we are entering; the other fills us to overflowing with a drink from the celestial life itself."

And I think the child was right.

When we emerged from the water, we found the banks of the lake almost deserted, everyone having gone, at the call of the bell, to their happy duties of the hour. Groups of children still ran around in joyful freedom. Some climbed the trees that hung over the water, with the agility of squirrels, and dropped with happy shouts of laughter into the lake, floating around on its surface like water lilies or lotus flowers.

"No fear of harm or danger; no dread or anxiety—only security and joy and peace! This is indeed the blessed life," I said, as we stood watching the happy children play.

"I often think how we were taught to believe that heaven was where we would wear crowns of gold and stand with harps always in our hands," Mae said, as we turned to go. "Our crowns of gold are the halos His blessed presence casts about us; and we do not need harps to accompany our songs of praise. We do see the crowns, and we do hear the angelic harps, when God wills it, but our best worship is to do His will."

"You are indeed wise in the ways of heaven, my child," I answered. "How happy I am to learn from one so dear to me! Tell me all about your life here."

So as we walked she told me the history of her years in heaven—her duties, her joys, her friends, her home—with all of her former enthusiasm. I learned that her home was distant from our own, far beyond the spires of the great city across the lake, but she added, "What is distance in heaven? We come and go at will. We feel no fatigue or haste, experience no delays—only blessings!"

Not far from our home we saw a group of children playing in the grass, and with them was a big, beautiful dog, over which they were rolling and tumbling with great abandon. As we approached he broke away from them and came bounding to meet us, crouching and fawning at my feet with every gesture of glad welcome.

"Do you not know him, auntie?" Mae asked.

"It's Sport!" I cried, stooping and placing my arms about his neck, and resting my head on his silken hair.

"Dear old fellow! How happy I am to have you here!"

He responded to my caresses with every expression of delight, and Mae laughed aloud at our mutual joy.

"I have often wondered if I would someday find him here. He surely deserves a happy life for his faithfulness and devotion in the other life. His intelligence and his fidelity were far above those of many human beings whom we count immortal."

"Didn't he sacrifice his life for little Will?"

"Yes; he tried to cross the track in front of an approaching train, because he saw it would pass between him and Will. It cost his life. He always placed himself between any of us and threatened danger, but he seemed to consider Will his special responsibility. He was a brave fellow—I am so glad to see him here. Dear Sport, you shall never leave me again!" I said, caressing him fondly.

At this he sprang to his feet, barking joyously, and ran and frolicked before us the rest of the way home, where he lay down on the doorstep, with an upward glance and a wag of his bushy tail, as though to say, "See how I take you at your word!"

"He understands every word we say," Mae laughed.

"Of course he does; he only lacks speech to make him perfect. I half hoped he might find it here."

"He would not be half so interesting if he could talk."

"Possibly not. How silken and beautiful his long hair is!"

"He has his bath in the river every day, and it leaves its mark on him also," she said. "Do you know, I think one of the sweetest proofs we have of the Father's loving care for us is that we so often find in this life the things that gave us great happiness below. The more unexpected they are, the greater joy it brings—I remember once seeing a beautiful little girl enter heaven, the very first of a large and affectionate family to come here. Later, I learned that her mother's sorrowful cry was, 'Oh, if only we had someone there to meet her, to care for her!' But she arrived lovingly nestled in the Master's own arms, and a little later, as He sat, still caressing and talking to her, a remarkably fine Angora kitten, of which the child had been very fond, and which had sickened and died some weeks before, came running across the grass and sprang directly into her arms, where it lay contentedly. Her glad cry as she recognized her little favorite, and the hugging and kissing that kitten received, added joy even in heaven! Who but our loving Father would have thought of such comfort for a little child?

"She had evidently been a timid child; but now as the other children gathered around her, with the delightful freedom they always manifest in the presence of Jesus, she, looking up confidingly into the tender eyes above her, began to shyly tell of the marvelous intelligence of her pet, until at last Jesus left her contentedly playing among the flowers with the others who had gathered around her. Our Father never forgets us, but provides pleasures and comforts for us all, according to our individual needs."

When shall I behold the Savior? When will I meet, face to face, the One my soul loves so? My hungry heart began to cry out from its depths.

Mae, as though understanding the silent cry, placed both her arms around my neck, looked tenderly into my eyes, and whispered, "You will see Him soon. He never delays when the time is ripe for His coming. It will not be long; you will see Him soon."

CHAPTER 8

The following morning Frank asked, after an hour of interesting instruction, "Would you like to go for the promised visit to Mrs. Wickham now?"

"Oh, yes!" I answered eagerly, and we left at once.

We soon reached her home and found her waiting at the entrance as though expecting us. After a cordial greeting, Frank said, "I will leave you together for that long talk I know you are both eager for. I will find you later on, at home."

"That's fine," I told him. "I'm familiar with the way now."

After Frank had gone, my friend showed me her home, pointing out with great pleasure the rooms that had been prepared for each beloved member still to come from her earthly household. One very large and inviting room, with blossom- and fruit-laden branches of the immortal trees shading its windows at each end, was evidently special to her; she whispered to me, "Douglass always did like a large room. I am sure he will like this one."

Returning down the broad stairway, we entered a very large music room, with broad galleries supported by marble columns running along three sides, on a level with the second floor. In this gallery were musical instruments—harps, cellos, basses, and some unlike any instruments I had ever seen before. The room itself was filled with easy chairs, couches, and window seats, where listeners could rest and listen to the music from the galleries.

"My daughter," my friend explained, "who left us in early childhood, has received excellent musical training here, and enjoys gathering her young friends and giving us a musical treat. You know our old home in Springville has furnished some rare voices for the heavenly choirs: Mary Allis, Will Griggs, and many others you will hear often in this room, I trust."

From this room, we reentered the dainty reception hall that opened to the front veranda and outer steps. Here Mrs. Wickham drew me to a seat beside her and said, "Now, tell me everything about our dear home and everyone there."

Holding hands as we talked—as I answered her questions—we spoke for hours of things too sacred to be repeated here. Standing suddenly, she said, "I must leave you for a little while—no, please stay," she added when I would have risen. "There is still a lot to talk about. Wait here, I will return."

I had already learned not to question the judgment of those who had been here longer, and I yielded to her wishes. As she passed through the doorway to the inner house, I saw a stranger at the front entrance and went to greet him. He was tall and commanding, with a face of great sweetness and beauty. Where had I seen him before? Surely I had met him since I came. *Ah, now I know!* I thought. *It is St. John, the beloved disciple.* He had been pointed out to me one morning by the riverside.

"Peace be unto this house," he said as he entered.

How his voice stirred and thrilled me! No wonder the Master loved him, with that voice and that face!

"Please come in. You are a welcome guest. I will call the mistress,"
I said.

"No, do not call her. She knows that I am here; she will return," he
said. "Sit here awhile with me," he continued, as he saw that I still stood,
after I had seated him. He got up and led me to a seat near him, and like
a child, I did as I was asked; still watching the wonderful face before me.

"Have you arrived here recently?" he asked.

"Yes, I have only been here a short time—so short that I don't know
not how to tell time as you count it here," I answered.

"Ah, that is not important," he reassured me with a gentle smile.
"Many here always cling to the language of earth. It is a link between the
two lives, and we would not want it any other way. How are you doing
with the change? What do you think of the life here?"

"Ah," I answered, "if those on earth could only know! I never fully
understood the meaning of that passage, 'No eye has seen, no ear has
heard, and no mind has imagined what God has prepared for those who
love him.'[13] It is indeed beyond human comprehension." I spoke with
deep feeling.

"'For those who love him'? Do you believe that all Christians truly
love him?" he asked. "Do you think they love the Father for the gift
of the Son and the Son because of the Father's love and mercy? Or do
they worship often out of duty rather than love?" He spoke reflectively
and gently.

"You who know the beloved Master so well—who were so loved by
Him—how can you doubt the love He must inspire in the hearts of all
who seek to know Him?" I replied

A radiant glow spread over the wonderful face, which He lifted, looking directly at me—the mist rolled away from my eyes and I knew Him!
With a low cry of joy and adoration, I threw myself at His feet, bathing

---

13   1 Corinthians 2:9.

them with happy tears. He gently stroked my bowed head for a moment, then rising, lifted me to His side.

"My Savior—my King!" I whispered, clinging closely to Him.

"Yes, and Elder Brother and Friend," He added, tenderly wiping away the tears from my eyes.

"Yes, yes,—' Chief among ten thousand,' and the One 'altogether lovely!'"[14] again I whispered.

"Ah, now you begin to meet the conditions of the new life! Like many others, the changing of faith to sight with you has produced a little shrinking, a little fear. That is all wrong. Have you forgotten the promise, 'I am going to prepare a place for you . . . so that you will always be with me where I am.'?[15] If you loved Me when you could only see Me by faith, love Me even more now when we really have become co-heirs of the Father. Come to Me with all that worries you or makes you glad; come to your Elder Brother, who is always waiting to receive you with joy."

Then He drew me to a seat, and conversed with me long and earnestly, unfolding many of the mysteries of the divine life. I hung on His words; I drank in every tone of His voice; I eagerly watched every line of His beloved face; and I was exalted, uplifted, beyond the power of words to express. Finally, with a divine smile, He stood to leave.

"We will meet often," He said, and I pressed my lips reverently to the hand still holding my own. Then, laying His hands a moment in blessing on my bowed head, He noiselessly and swiftly left the house.

As I stood watching the Savior's fast-receding figure passing beneath the flower-laden trees, I saw two beautiful young girls approaching where He went. With arms intertwined they were happily conversing together: Mary Bates and Mae Camden. When they saw the Master, they flew to meet Him with a glad cry, and as He extended a hand to each, they

14   Song of Solomon 5:10, 16 (NKJV).
15   John 14:2–3.

turned, and clinging to His hand, one on either side, they went with Him, looking up trustingly into His face as He talked with them, and apparently chatting with Him freely.

I saw His face in profile whenever He turned and looked down lovingly on one or the other of them, and I thought, *That is the way He wants us to be with Him—really like children with a beloved older brother.* I watched until the trees hid them from sight, longing to call the dear girls to me, but knowing His presence meant more to them than anything else; and at last I turned and passed softly through the house to the beautiful entrance at the rear.

Just before I reached the door I met my friend Mrs. Wickham. Before I could speak, she said, "I know all about it. Do not try to speak; I know your heart is full. I will see you very soon—go home now!" And with that, she pushed me gently to the door.

How my heart blessed her—for it seemed disrespectful indeed to try to talk of ordinary topics after this blessed experience. I did not follow the walk, but went across the flowery turf, beneath the trees, till I reached home. I found Frank sitting on the veranda, and as I ascended the steps he rose to meet me. When he saw my face, he took both my hands in his for an instant, and simply said, very gently, "Ah, I see you have been with the Master!" Then he stepped aside so I could enter the house.

I hurried to my room, where I closed the draperies behind me at the door, then threw myself onto the couch, and with closed eyes relived every instant I had spent in that hallowed Presence. I recalled every word and tone of the Savior's voice, and committed the instructions He had given me indelibly to my memory. I seemed to have been lifted to a higher plane of existence, to have drunk deeply from the fountain of all good, since I had met Him. It was a long, blessed communion that I held with my own soul on that special day. When I looked on the pictured face above me, I was amazed that I had not at once recognized the Christ;

the likeness was so perfect. But I concluded that for some wise purpose I could not know Him until it He knew that I was ready to see Him as He is.

It was twilight when I rose at last, and I knelt by my couch, intending to offer my first prayer in heaven. Up to this time my life there had been a constant thanksgiving—there had seemed no room for petition. But as I knelt, I could only say over and over, "I thank You, blessed Father; I thank You, I thank You!"

When I descended the stairs at last, I found my brother-in-law standing in the flower room, and, going to him, I asked, "Frank, what do you do in heaven when you want to pray?"

"We praise!" he answered.

"Then let's praise now," I said.

So standing there with clasped hands, we lifted up our hearts and voices in a hymn of praise to God, my brother leading with his clear, strong voice, I following. As the first notes sounded, I thought the roof echoed them; but I soon realized that other voices blended with ours, until the whole house seemed filled with unseen singers. Earth never heard such a grand hymn of praise! And as the hymn went on, I recognized many dear voices from the past—Will Griggs's pathetic tenor, Mary Allis's exquisite soprano, and many other voices that wakened memories of long ago. Then I heard sweet child voices and, looking up, I saw above us a cloud of radiant baby faces that flooded my heart with joy. The room seemed filled with them.

"Oh, what a divine life!" I whispered when, after standing until the last lingering notes had died away, Frank and I returned to the veranda and sat in the golden twilight.

"You are only in the first pages of its record," he said. "Its blessedness must be gradually unfolded to us, or we could not bear its dazzling glory—even here."

Then followed an hour of instruction, when he led my soul still deeper into the mysteries of the glorious life I had now entered. He taught and I listened. Sometimes I questioned, but rarely. I was content to receive the heavenly manna as it was given to me, with a heart full of gratitude and love.

CHAPTER 9

The next day, my brother was away on an important mission, so I started out alone to see if I could find the dear young friends I had caught only a fleeting glimpse of the day before. I knew that all things happened as they should in that happy world, and that sooner or later I would find them again; yet I couldn't help hoping it might be very soon. I recalled the happy light on their fresh young faces when they met the Master, and I longed to talk with them about their day-to-day life.

I soon began again to recall my blessed interview with Jesus, and became so absorbed in these thoughts that I was even oblivious to the beautiful world around me.

Suddenly I heard someone say, "Surely that is Mrs. Sprague!" and looking up I saw Mary Bates a few steps away, regarding me intently. I cried joyfully, "My precious Mamie!"

She flew to me, and folding me in her arms, drew my head to her shoulder, almost sobbing in her great joy. "Muzzer!"—a pet name she often used in our happy past—"how very glad I am to have you here! I could scarcely wait to find you."

"How did you know I was here, Mamie?"

"The Master told me," she said softly. "Mae had already told me, and we were on the way to find you when we met Him, and He told us He had just left you. Then we knew we must wait a little."

How my heart thrilled! He had thought about, had spoken of me, after we parted! I longed to ask her what He had said, but dared not. Seeming to divine my thoughts, she continued:

"He spoke so tenderly about you, and said we must stay with you as much as we can. Mae had work to do today, and since she had already seen you once, I came alone. She may be here later on. May I stay a long time with you? There is so much to tell you, so much to ask about!"

"Indeed you may. I had started out to find you, when we met. Come on, let's go home at once." So, holding hands, we set out toward my home. "What shall I tell you first?"

"Everything about my dear ones—every individual member of our beloved household. Begin with my precious, heartbroken mother"—her voice broke a little, but she soon continued. "I go to her often, but her great sorrow keeps her from receiving the comfort I long to give her. If she could only one hour with me here, and know God's wisdom and love as we know it, I am certain the cloud would lift from her life! She would see that what we thought of there as two lives—earthly and heavenly—are, after all, only one."

"Yes, dear," I answered, "I urged her to think of it that way and to trust in the Father's tender care and unfailing love—but it is difficult on earth to see beyond the lonely heart and the vacant chair. Still, I believe she is beginning to understand and be ready to receive the comfort you are so eager to give."

"Ah, if only she knew how that would complete my happiness now! We cannot grieve here as we did on earth, because we have learned to accept that the will of the Father is always tender and wise; but even heaven can never be complete for me while I know that my precious mother is forgetting her many blessings, simply because I am not with her, in the flesh, to share them. There is my father, and the boys—why, I am as truly hers still as they are, if she only knew it! I often sit with them all, holding her hand in mine, or my arms about her—my dear little mother! Why does she need to see me, to understand this? But I am almost complaining, aren't I? Some day she will know—I must be patient."

We walked on slowly, talking about life on earth, still so near to us in many ways. She asked eager questions, and I answered them as best I could.

We soon noticed three women and a man standing under the trees a little to one side of the walk. The man's back was toward us, but we recognized the Master at once. The women were all strangers, and one of them seemed to have just arrived. The Savior held her hand as He talked with her, and they all listened intently to His words. We regarded the group in silence as we passed, not hoping for recognition from him at such a time, but just as we were opposite them, He turned and looked at us. He did not speak—but oh, that look! It was so full of tenderness and encouragement and blessing! It lifted us upward, it enthralled and exalted us; and as we passed on, our clasped hands tightened, and unspeakable joy flooded our hearts.

We finished our walk in silence, and sat down on the marble steps in the shadow of the overhanging trees outside my house. The dear child nestled close to me, and laid her head on my shoulder, while I rested my cheek on her head. After a time I whispered, half to myself, "Was there ever such a look!"

Instantly she raised her head and looked at me, saying eagerly, "You think so too? I was sure you would. It is always that way: if He is too occupied to speak to you at the time, He just looks at you, and it is as though He had talked with you a long while. He is so wonderful! Why couldn't we know Him on earth as we do here?"

"How long were you here before you met Him?" I asked her.

"Oh, that is the wonderful part of it! His was the first face I saw after I left my earthly body. I felt confused when I first realized I was free, and I just stood there, not knowing what to do. Then I saw Him standing right beside me, with that same look on His face. At first I felt shy and half afraid. But then He stretched out his hand to me, and said, 'My child, I have come to take care of you. Trust Me; do not be afraid.' That was when I recognized Him, and instantly all fear left me. I clung to Him like He was one of my brothers. He did not say much to me, but somehow I felt that He understood all of my thoughts. After a moment, I asked Him, 'May I stay awhile with Mama? She is heartbroken.'

"'Yes, dear child, you may stay as long as you desire,' He answered and I could see the compassion in His eyes.

"'Will You stay too?' I asked, because I already felt I could not bear to have Him leave me.

"He looked so pleased, as though He knew my thoughts, and He answered, 'Yes, I will stay with you, until you are ready to come with Me.'

"Then I went to Mama and put my arms around her, and soon the Master came too, and whispered words of comfort to her; but I am not sure she felt our presence, though I believed that she seemed calmer with my caresses. We stayed until everything was over and I never left Mama for an instant, except twice I went to poor little Hal's sickroom when he was alone for a short time. I have always felt that he recognized my presence more than any of them, because he lay so still and calm when I talked to him. He seemed to be listening.

"When they gathered for the last time around my casket, I wanted so badly to speak, to show myself to them! If they could have for just one instant seen me alive, standing so calmly in their midst, surely they would have turned away from the lifeless clay they had embalmed and beautified for the tomb. They would have finally known I was not there—but they just would not recognize the truth. At last I pleaded with the Master to let me show myself to them, just once. But He said, 'It is not the Father's will.'

"After that I fully accepted the Father's will, and soon the Master brought me here in His arms. And what a blessed life it is here!"

I can only give a brief outline here of our conversation on that first day. Much of it is too sacred to be scanned by curious eyes. We talked until the golden twilight fell, and we watched the little birds nestling in the vines, and heard in the distance the solemnly joyful notes of the angels' choral song, and joined our own voices in their hymn of praise. Later we went to my room, and lay down on my dainty couch for a rest, and the last words I heard before sinking into heaven's blissful sleep were her tenderly whispered, "Dear, dear little Muzzer, I am so happy that you are here!"

More than once I have been asked, "Was there night there?" Emphatically, no! What, for want of a better designation, we might call "day," was full of a glorious radiance, a rosy golden light, which was everywhere. There is no language known on earth that can describe its marvelous glory. It flooded the sky; it was caught up and reflected in the waters; it filled all of heaven with joy and all hearts with song. After a period much longer than our longest earthly day, this glory mellowed and softened until it became a glowing, peaceful twilight. The children ceased their playing beneath the trees, the little birds nestled among the vines, and all who had been busy in various ways throughout the day sought rest and quiet. But there was no darkness, no dusky shadows even—only a restful softening of the glory.

CHAPTER 10

O ne day not long after my visit with Mary Bates, Frank said, "We will go to the grand auditorium this morning; it will be a rare day even here. Martin Luther is to speak on 'The Reformation: Its Causes and Effects,' followed by a talk from John Wesley. There may also be other speakers."

It was not the first time we had visited this great auditorium, though I have not described it before now. The building stood upon a slight elevation, and massive columns of amethyst and jasper supported its mighty dome. The vast structure had no walls, only the great dome and supporting columns.

A broad platform of precious marble rose from the center; it was inlaid with a dark-red stone with embedded crystals that caught and reflected the light. On three sides of the platform, tiered seats of highly polished cedar formed an immense amphitheater. At the back of the platform were heavy hangings of royal purple, and an altar of solid pearl stood near the center.

The great dome was deep and dark in its immensity, so that only the golden statues around its lower border were distinctly visible. I had noticed all these details during previous visits.

When we entered on this day, we found the building filled with people eagerly waiting to hear the speakers. Soon we were seated and also waiting. Soft strains of music floated around us from an invisible choir, and we didn't wait long before Martin Luther, in the prime of a vigorous manhood, ascended the steps and stood before us. It is not my purpose to dwell upon his appearance, except to say that his great intellect and spiritual strength seemed to have added to his already powerful physique, and made him a fit leader still, even in heavenly places.

Luther's message alone would fill a book, and even an outline would be too much to include here. His eloquence and powerful presence captured our attention.

When Luther finished, John Wesley took his place. The saintly beauty of Wesley's face, intensified by the heavenly light that shone on it, was a wonder to behold. His theme was "God's Love"; and if on earth he spoke powerfully on the subject, in heaven the fire of his exalted prose ignited our souls, until we softened like wax in his hands. He showed what that divine love had done for us, and how an eternity of thanksgiving and praise could never repay it.

The whole auditorium was silent for some time after he left, except for the faint melody of the unseen choir. The audience seemed lost in contemplation of the message so tenderly delivered. Then the heavy curtains at the back of the platform parted, and a tall form, on whom all the glory of heaven seemed to center, emerged and advanced toward the middle of the platform. Instantly the vast congregation of souls rose to their feet, and burst forth with one voice in that grand anthem we had so often sung on earth:

> All hail the power of Jesus' name,
> Let angels prostrate fall;

Bring forth the royal diadem,
And crown him Lord of all.

Such a grand chorus of voices, such unity, such harmony, such volume, was never heard on earth. It rose, it swelled, it seemed to fill not only the great auditorium, but heaven itself. And still, above it all, we heard the voices of the angel choir, no longer breathing the soft, sweet melody, but bursting forth in triumphant praise. A flood of glory seemed to fill the place, and looking up, we saw the dome ablaze with golden light, and the angelic forms of the no longer invisible choir in its midst, with their heavenly harps and viols, and their faces only a little less radiant than that of the One whose praise they sang. And He, before whom all heaven bowed in adoration, stood with uplifted face and kingly demeanor, the very God of earth and heaven. He is the center and the Source of all light, and a divine radiance surrounded Him that is impossible to describe.

As the hymn of praise and adoration ceased, we all sank slowly to our knees, every head bowed and every face covered as the angel choir chanted the familiar words:

Glory be to the Father,
and to the Son,
and to the Holy Ghost.
As it was in the beginning,
is now, and ever shall be,
world without end.
Amen, Amen!

As the voices slowly died away, a holy silence fell on us. Presently, slowly and reverently, we all rose and resumed our places—no, not all. Sweet Mary Bates had accompanied us to the sanctuary, and I now noticed that she alone still knelt in our midst, with clasped hands and radiant uplifted face, her eyes fixed upon the Savior as He stood waiting before us, with such a look of self-forgetful adoration and love that she herself appeared truly divine. I dared not disturb her; but in a moment the Master turned and met her adoring eyes with a look of loving recognition, and with a deep sigh of satisfied desire she quietly resumed her seat beside me, slipping her little hand into mine with all the confidence of a child who feels unconditionally loved and understood.

As I looked at the glorious form before us, clothed in all the majesty of the Godhead, I tremblingly wondered: *Can this really be the Christman Pilate condemned to die a despicable death on the cross?* It seemed impossible that anyone, however vile, could be blind to the divinity so plainly revealed in Him.

Then the Savior began to speak, and the sweetness of His voice was far beyond the melody of the heavenly choir. And His gracious words!— earth has no language by which I could convey their meaning. He first touched lightly upon earthly life, and taught us how the two lives—past and present—are linked. Then He unfolded some of the mysteries of the heavenly life, and pointed out the joyful duties before us.

When He finished speaking, we sat with bowed heads as He withdrew from us. We were so uplifted, so filled with His holy presence, that we left the place silently and reverently, each with a heart filled with higher, more divine aspirations, and clearer views of the blessed life we had begun.

I can only touch lightly on these heavenly joys. There is a depth and mystery to everything about the divine life that I dare not try to describe. It is too holy to be exposed casually. Suffice it to say, that any joy we know on earth, however rare or sacred, is less than the faintest shadow of the joy of even one moment in heaven. There is no sorrow; no pain; no sickness; no death; no partings; no disappointments; no tears but those of joy; no broken hopes; no mislaid plans; no night, no storm, no shadows—only light and joy and love and peace and rest forever and forever. My soul whispers reverently, amen and amen.

CHAPTER 11

As the days passed I went frequently to the sacred lake, sometimes alone, sometimes with one or more of my own family circle, or with friends. It was always an inspiring and uplifting experience. It never became routine enough to overcome the great awe I felt on my visit; but I found that the more often I bathed or floated and slept in its crystal-clear current, the stronger I grew in spirit, and the more clearly I understood the mysteries of heaven.

My almost daily encounters with dear ones from whom I had long been separated on earth served to restore to me the feeling of home that was the greatest comfort in my mortal life, and I began to realize that heaven was indeed the true life, instead of that probationary life which we had always regarded as real.

I think it was the day after I returned from my first visit to earth, that, as I started to cross the lawn between my father's house and our own, I heard my name called in affectionate tones. I turned and saw a tall, fine-looking man approaching me; his hair was silvery white, and his deep-blue eyes looked happily and tenderly into mine, as he drew near.

"Oliver!" I cried, reaching out to him, "Dear, dear Oliver!" He was the husband of my oldest sister.

"I did not know that you had come, until a few moments ago, when your father told me. It is delightful to have you here; it seems more like the old life to see you than any of the others who are here, because we were together so much during my last years on earth," he said, grasping my hands warmly. "Where are you going now? Can you not come with me for a while? I was thinking only a few days ago how much I wished you could be here to help me before Lu came; you know her tastes so well. And now here you are! So often even our unspoken wishes are granted in heaven!"

"Is my sister coming soon?" I asked him a little later.

"That I cannot say with confidence; but you know the years on earth are passing, and it can't be much longer. Can you come with me now?"

"Gladly," I said, turning to walk with him.

"It is only a little way from here," he said, "just where the river bends. Lu loves the water, so I chose that spot in preference to one nearer your home."

"This is truly enchanting!" I cried, as we drew near the place. "I have not been this way before."

"I want you to see the view of the river from her room," he said. "I know you will enjoy it."

We entered the truly beautiful house, built of the purest white granite, and nestled in the foliage of the flower-laden trees so that from some points only glimpses of it were visible.

"Lu loves flowers so much—won't she enjoy these trees?" he asked with almost boyish delight.

"She will," I agreed.

We passed through several delightful rooms on the lower floor, and ascended the stairway, which in itself was a dream of beauty. When we entered the room he was so anxious for me to see, I stopped on the threshold with an exclamation of delight, while he stood watching the expression on my face with keen enjoyment.

"It is the most delightful room I ever saw!"

The framework of the couches, chairs, and desk was of pure and spotless pearl; they were upholstered in dim gold. There were soft rugs and draperies accenting the room. A low window, opening onto the flower-wreathed balcony, framed so enchanting a view of the broad, smooth river below, that again I caught my breath in delight. The tranquil waters reflected a thousand exquisite tints from the heavens above, and a boat floating on the current was perfectly mirrored in the iridescent ripples. Far across the shining waters, domes and pillared temples and sparkling fountains dotted the celestial hills. When at last I turned from this entrancing view, I saw on the opposite wall, smiting down on me, the same divine face that I daily looked upon in my own room at home.

We descended the stairs without a word, and even then I could only falter, "Only heaven could offer such perfection in everything!"

Oliver pressed my hand sympathetically, and I left without another word.

Many months, by earthly time, had passed since that day, and many times I had gone to that lovely home and visited with my beloved brother-in-law. I could suggest nothing that would add to the beauty of the place, but we planned for and anticipated the joy of her coming.

One day I found him absent, and though I waited a long time, he did not return. I hadn't seen him for several days, and concluded the Master had sent him on some mission. Walking home, I met a group of happy young girls and boys, of different ages, hurrying in the direction I was coming from, with their arms full of beautiful flowers. As they drew near I recognized the grandchildren of my dear sister—Stanley and Mary and David and Lee and little Ruth. As soon as they saw me, they began to shout joyfully, "Grandma is coming! Grandma is coming! We are taking flowers for her! We can hardly wait!"

"How do you know she's coming? I have just come from the house—no one is there."

"But she is coming," Lee told me with assurance. "We had a message from Grandpa, and he is bringing her."

"Then I will tell the others, and we will all come to welcome her."

With great joy in my heart I hurried to my parents' house and found them waiting for me, full of joyful expectation.

"Yes, we also have had word," my father said, "and were only waiting for your return, so that we could go together."

"Then I will go get Frank, so he can come with us," I said.

"I am here!" said a genial voice and, looking up, I saw him at the door.

"Col. Sprague is always present when he is needed," said my father cordially.

So we all set forth—my father, my mother, and my sister Jodie; my brother the doctor and his two fair daughters; my Aunt Gray, her son Martin, and his wife and daughter; my brother-in-law Frank and I—to welcome this dearly loved one to her eternal home.

As we approached the house we heard the sound of joyful voices, and looking in, we saw my sister standing in the room, her husband's arm around her, and the happy grandchildren flitted around them like hummingbirds among the flowers.

But what was this? Could this radiant creature, with her smooth brow and happy eyes, be the pale, worn woman I had last seen bowed with suffering and sorrow? I looked with eager eyes. Yes, it was my sister; but as she was thirty years earlier, with the bloom of health on her face, and the light of youth in her eyes. I drew back into the shadow of the vines and let the others precede me, for my heart was full of a strange, triumphant joy. This surely was the "victory over death"[16] promised by our risen Lord. I watched the happy greetings, and the way she took each loved one into her arms. When she had greeted and embraced them all, I saw her turn and look wistfully around, then whisper to my father, "Isn't my little sister here?"

I could wait no longer, but hurried to her side, calling, "Dearest, I am here! Welcome!"

She held me fast in her warm embrace and showered my face with kisses, while I laughed and cried for joy that she had come at last. Oh, what a family reunion that was! Its bliss was heightened by the sure knowledge (not the hope) that there would be no more partings for us, ever again!

My brother-in-law Oliver looked on with proud and happy eyes. The hour for which he had longed and waited had finally come and his home life was now complete forevermore. I told him how I had waited for him earlier, and he said, "We saw you as you left the house, but were too far away to call you. I had taken her into the river, and she saw the house and admired it greatly before she knew it was our home."

"What did she do when she saw her lovely room?"

"Cried like a child, and clung to me, and said, 'This more than repays us for the home we left on earth!' If the children hadn't come, I think she would still be standing at that window!" he said, laughing happily.

"I am glad you had her all to yourself at first," I whispered. "You deserved that happiness, if any man ever did."

He smiled gratefully, and looked over at his wife, where she stood at the center of a happy group.

"Doesn't she look very young to you, Oliver?" I asked.

"The years peeled off her face like a mask, as we sat beneath the water in the river. We all renew our youth in those life-giving waters, but she

16   1 Corinthians 15:57

became at once unusually fair and young."

"Her coming has made you younger too," I said, noting his fresh complexion and his sparkling eyes, "but I hope it will not change your silver hair, for that is like a crown of glory."

He looked at me a moment critically, then said, "I wonder if you realize the change that has likewise come to you in this wonderful place?"

"To me?" I said, a little startled at the thought. "I confess I have not once thought of my personal appearance. I realize what, through the Father's mercy, this life has done for me spiritually, but I have never given an instant's thought to the physical change."

"The change is every bit as great in your case as in Lu's, though with you the change has been more gradual," he said.

I felt a strange thrill of joy that when my dear husband arrived, he would find me as I was in our early years together. It was a sweet thought, and my heart was full of gratitude to the Father for this further evidence of his loving care.

We talked together and the hours sped by, until at last my father said, "Come, children; we must not forget that this dear daughter of mine needs rest on this first day in her new home."

So with light hearts we went our way, and left them to spend their first hours in heaven together.

CHAPTER 12

After we left my parents and friends on our return from welcoming my sister, Frank hurried away on some mission, and I walked on alone toward the sacred lake. I felt the need of a rest in its soothing waters after the morning's activities. I normally visited the lake in the early morning hours; it was now past noon of the heavenly day, and only a few persons lingered on the shore. The boats that sped across its calm surface seemed to be filled with those intent upon some duty rather than with pleasure seekers.

I walked slowly down into the water, and soon found myself floating, as usual, in mid current. The wonderful prismatic rays that in the early morning were such a marvel, now blended into a golden glory, with shades of rose and purple flashing across their splendor. To me it seemed even more beautiful than the rainbow tints; just as the more mature joys of earthly life cast into shadow the fleeting pleasures of youth. It made me wonder what its evening glories would be, and I resolved to come at some glowing twilight, and see if it reminded me of the calm hours of earth's sunset.

The chimes from the silver bell in the great city were ringing an anthem as I lay, and its notes seemed to chant clearly, "Holy! Holy! Holy! Lord God Almighty!" The waters took up the song and a thousand waves about me responded, "Holy! Holy! Holy!"

The notes seemed to vibrate upon the waves, producing a wondrously harmonious effect. The front row in the battalion of advancing waves softly chanted "Holy" as it passed onward. Immediately the second row of waves took up the word that the first seemed to have dropped as it echoed the second "Holy" in the divine chorus; then it, too, passed onward to take up the second note as the third advancing column caught the first—and so it passed and echoed from wave to wave, until it seemed millions of tiny waves about me had taken up and were bearing their part in this grand crescendo. Language fails me: I cannot hope to convey to others this experience. It was overpowering. I lay and listened until my whole being was filled with the divine melody, and I seemed to be part of the great chorus, and then I lifted up my voice and joined the thrilling song of praise.

I found that, unlike my usual habit, I floated rapidly away from the shore where I had entered the water, and after a time realized that I was approaching a portion of the lakeshore I had never yet visited. Refreshed and invigorated, I ascended the sloping banks, to find myself in the midst of a lovely suburban village, similar to the one where our own home was situated. The architecture and construction of the houses was somewhat different here, but they were no less beautiful than others I had seen. Many were constructed of polished woods, and somewhat resembled the finest chalets in Switzerland, though far surpassing them in artistry.

As I wandered on, feasting my eyes on the lovely views, I was particularly pleased by the appearance of an unusually attractive house. Its broad verandas almost overhung the waters of the lake, with wide low steps running on one side of the house down to the water's edge. Several graceful swans were leisurely drifting about with the current, and a bird similar to our southern mockingbird, but with softer voice, was singing in the low branches overhead. There were many larger and more imposing villas nearby, but I found none of them as charming as this sweet home.

I saw a woman sitting beneath one of the large flowering trees next to the cottage. With her delicate hands, she was weaving a snow-white gossamer fabric that fell in a soft fleecy heap at her side as the work progressed. She was so very small in stature that at first glance I thought she was a child; but a closer scrutiny showed her to be a mature woman, though with the glow of youth still upon her smooth cheek. Something familiar in her gestures, rather than her appearance, made me feel that it was not the first time we had met; and growing accustomed now to the delightful surprises that met me everywhere in this world of rare delights, I drew near to greet her. Before I could speak, she looked up.

"Maggie!" "Mrs. Sprague dear!" we cried simultaneously, and, dropping her work from her hands, she stood up quickly to greet me.

Our greeting was warm, and her sweet face glowed with a welcome that reminded me of the happy days when we had met, a long time ago, by the shore of that other beautiful lake in our earthly life.

"Now I know why I came this way today—to find you!" I said, as we sat side by side, talking as we never talked on earth—for the shyness of her mortal life had melted away in the balmy air of heaven.

"What is this lovely fabric you are weaving?" I presently asked, lifting the silken fleecy web in my fingers as I spoke.

"Some draperies for Nellie's room," she said. "You know we two have lived alone together so much, I thought it would seem more like home to her—to us both—if we did the same here. So this cottage is our own special home, just a step from Marie's." She pointed to an imposing house a few yards distant. "I am fitting it up as daintily as I can, especially her room."

"Oh, let me help you!" I said. "It would be such a pleasure to me."

She hesitated an instant, with something of her former shyness, then said: "That is so like you, dear Mrs. Sprague. I have my heart set on doing Nellie's room entirely myself—there is no hurry about it, you know—but if you really would enjoy it, I would love to have you help me in the other rooms."

"And will you teach me how to weave these delicate hangings?"

"Yes, indeed. Shall I give you your first lesson now?"

Lifting the dainty thread, she showed me how to toss and wind it through my fingers till it fell away in shining folds. It was very light and fascinating work, and I soon was weaving it almost as rapidly as she did.

Now I can help Carroll! I thought happily, as I saw the shimmering fabric grow beneath my hands. *Tomorrow I will go and show him how beautifully we can drape the doors and windows.*

In heaven our first thought always is to give pleasure to others.

"You are a good student," said Maggie, laughing happily, "and what a charming hour you have given me!"

"I have thoroughly enjoyed it," I answered. "I am glad we met again."

I left with the understanding that I was to repeat the visit. When I urged her to also visit me, her shyness again appeared, as she said, "Oh, they are all strangers to me, and here we will be entirely alone. You come to me."

So I yielded; in heaven we never pressure anyone to consent to something they are reluctant to do, however much we may want it. We spent many happy hours together in the cottage by the lake.

CHAPTER 13

On another of my many walks at this time, I came upon a scene that brought to mind what Mae had said about the Savior's love for little children.[17] I found Him sitting beneath one of the flowering trees at the lakeshore, with about a dozen children of all ages gathered around Him. One dainty tot, not more than a year old, was nestled in His arms, with her sunny head resting confidingly upon His chest, her tiny hands filled with the lovely water lilies that floated everywhere on the waters. She was too young to realize how great her privilege was, but seemed to be enjoying His care to the utmost. The others sat at His feet, or leaned on His knees; and one little fellow with earnest eyes stood by Him, leaning on His shoulder, while the Master's right arm encircled Him. Every eye was fixed eagerly on Jesus, and each child appeared alert to catch every word He said. He seemed to be telling them some very absorbing story, adapted to their childish tastes and understanding.

I sat down on the grass among a group of people, a little removed from the children, and tried to hear what He was saying, but we were too far away to catch more than a sentence now and then, and in heaven

17   Matthew 19:14

one never intrudes upon another's privileges or pleasures. So we simply enjoyed the smiles and eager questions and exclamations of the children, and gathered a little of the story from the disjointed sentences which floated to us.

"A little child lost in the dark woods of the lower world," we heard the Master say, in response to the inquiring looks of the interested children. "Lions and bears—" came later on.

"Where was his papa?" asked an anxious voice.

We could not hear the reply, but soon a little fellow leaning on the Savior's knee said confidently, "No lions and bears up here!"

"No," He replied, "nothing to harm or frighten my little children here."

Then as the story deepened and grew in interest, and the children pressed more closely about the Master, He turned with a sweet smile to the little fellow with the earnest eyes who leaned upon His shoulder, and asked, "What would you have done then, Leslie?"

With a bright light in his eyes and a flush on his fair cheek, the child answered quickly and emphatically, "I would have prayed to You and asked You to close the lion's mouth, like You did for Daniel, and You would have done it!"[18]

Ah, I thought, *if his parents could see the look the Master gave their son as He replied, they would be comforted even in the absence of their darling boy.*

Lost in my thoughts, I heard no more, until a happy shout from the little folks proclaimed how satisfactorily the story had ended. Looking up, I saw the Savior passing onward, with the baby still in His arms, and the children trooping about Him.

"The Kingdom of Heaven belongs to those who are like these children."[19] How much He loved them!

18   Daniel 6.
19   Matthew 19:14.

I rose and started homeward. I had not gone far before I met Frank, who greeted me with an invitation: "I am on my way to the city by the lake; will you accompany me?"

"I have wanted to visit the city. I was only waiting until you thought I was ready," I answered.

"You are growing so fast in knowledge of the heavenly ways," he said, "that I think I could take you almost anywhere with me now. You acquire the knowledge for the very love of it; not because you think it's your duty to learn what we want you to learn. Your eagerness to learn for yourself all truth, and at the same time your patience in waiting, often when I know it is difficult, have won for you much praise and love from our dear Master, who eagerly watches how we all progress in the divine life. I think it is only right to tell you this; we need encouragement here as well as we did on earth, though in a different way. I tell you this by divine permission. I think it will not be long before He trusts you with a mission; but I am telling you this myself, not at His command."

It would be impossible for me to convey, in the language of earth, the impression these words of commendation made on me. They were so unexpected. I had gone about, as Frank said, eagerly gathering the knowledge imparted to me, with a genuine love for the study of all things pertaining to heavenly life, without a thought that I in any way deserved to be commended for doing so; and now I had won the approval of the Master Himself! The happiness seemed almost more than I could bear, and I stopped suddenly and looked up into Frank's face with grateful tears.

"I am so glad for you!" he said, warmly clasping my hand. "You see, there are rewards in heaven; it does my soul good that you have unconsciously won one of them so soon."

I wish I could record in detail the precious words of wisdom that he spoke; I wish that I could recount in greater detail the events of that wonderful life as it unfolded day by day—but some things I am not permitted to share. When I undertook to write about that never-to-be-forgotten experience, I did not realize how many serious difficulties I would encounter, how often I would have to pause and consider if I might really reveal this truth or paint that scene as it appeared to me. The very heart has often been left out of some wonderful scene I was attempting to describe, because I found I dared not reveal its sacred secret. I realize painfully that the narrative, as I am forced to give it, falls infinitely short of what I hoped to make it when I began. But bear with me: it is no fanciful tale I am weaving, but an account of the true life beyond, as I experienced it when my exalted spirit rose triumphant over my wasted flesh, nearly destroyed by suffering.

Frank and I walked slowly back to the edge of the lake, where we stepped into a boat lying near the shore, and were at once transported to the farther shore, landing on a marble terrace at the entrance to the city by the lake. I never knew by what power these boats were propelled. The one in which we crossed the water had no oarsmen, no engine, no sails; but it moved steadily onward until we were reached our destination. The boat was fitted with luxuriously cushioned seats, and upon one of them lay a musical instrument something like a violin, although it no bow, but seemed to be played by the fingers alone.

On another seat lay a book, which I picked up and opened; it seemed to be a continuation of the book that has stirred and thrilled millions of hearts on earth, *The Greatest Thing in the World*. As I glanced through it while we journeyed, I understood the truth that Henry Drummond's great mind already had grappled with the mighty things of eternity and was providing food to immortals, even as he had to those in mortal life.

I was stirred from my thoughts by the boat touching the marble terrace, and found my brother already standing and waiting to assist me to the shore. We walked up a slight slope, and found ourselves in a broad street that led into the heart of the city. The streets were all very broad and smooth, and paved with marble and precious stones of every kind. Though they were thronged with people intent on various duties, not an atom of debris, or even dust, was visible anywhere.

There seemed to be large office buildings of many kinds, though I saw nothing resembling the retail establishments on earth. There were colleges and schools; book and music stores and publishing houses; and several large factories, which were where the many colors of fine silken threads were spun that were so extensively used in the weaving of the draperies I have already mentioned. There were art galleries, libraries, and many lecture halls and vast auditoriums.

But I saw no churches of any kind. At first this somewhat confused me, until I remembered that there are no religions in heaven; all worship together in harmony and love—the children of one loving Father. *Ah*, I thought, *what a pity that fact, if no other in heaven, could not be proclaimed to the inhabitants of earth! Surely that knowledge would do away with the petty contentions, jealousies, and rivalries of the militant church! No dogma in heaven! No controverted points of doctrine! No charges of heresy brought by one professed Christian against another! No building up of one denomination upon the ruins or downfall of a different sect! But one great universal brotherhood whose head is Christ, and whose cornerstone is Love.*

I thought of the day we had listened in the great auditorium to the divine address of our beloved Master, of the bowed heads and uplifted voices of that vast multitude as every voice joined to sing, "Crown him Lord of all!" I could have wept to think of the faces that must someday be bowed in shame when they remembered how often in mortal life they rejected another Christian, saying in actual words or in effect, "My way is the true path to God!"

We found no houses anywhere in the center of the city, but there were magnificent homes in the suburbs. One pleasing fact was that every home had a large yard, full of trees and flowers and pleasant walks; indeed, everywhere outside of the business center of the town was like one vast park. There was much that charmed and surprised me in this great city, of which I may not fully speak, but which I never can forget.

We found in one place a very large park, with walks and drives and fountains and miniature lakes and shaded seats, but no dwellings or buildings of any kind, except an immense circular open tabernacle capable of seating several hundred, where, Frank told me, a seraph choir assembled at a certain hour daily to sing the oratorios written by the great musical composers of earth and heaven. It had just departed, and the crowd that had enjoyed its divine music still lingered as though loath to leave a spot so hallowed.

"We will remember the hour," Frank said, "and come again when we can hear them."

CHAPTER 14

Passing through the park, we came out to open country, and walked some distance through flowery meadows and undulating plains. After awhile we entered a vast forest whose great trees towered above us like swaying giants. The day was nearly gone—a day so full of joy and glad surprises and happy hours! Full as it had been, I felt there was still something left, hidden deep in the twilight of the day, something that held my soul in awe, as if I were about to receive the holy sacrament.

Frank walked beside me, absorbed in silent thought, but with a touch beyond even his usual gentleness. I didn't ask where we were going at that unusual hour, so far from home, because fear and doubt and questioning no longer disturbed the my soul's peace. The forest was dense, but the golden glow of the twilight rested beneath the trees, sifting down through the quivering branches overhead as though falling through the windows of some grand cathedral.

We finally emerged from the forest, onto a vast plain that stretched to the horizon before us, and far away we faintly heard the thunder of the breaking waves in that immortal sea of which I had heard so much but had not yet seen. The silence was intense, except for the faint and distant echo of the waves. We stood a moment at the edge of the forest, then as we advanced a few steps into the plain I became aware that immediately to our right the ground rose into quite an elevation; and, turning toward it, I beheld a sight that all the years of earth and heaven's eternity can never erase.

On the summit of this gentle slope stood a temple, whose vast dome, massive pillars, and solid walls were of unsullied pearl; through its great mullioned windows shone a white radiance that swallowed up the golden glow of the twilight. I did not cry out or hide my face, as I had at other revelations.; I sank slowly to my knees and, crossing my hands on my breast, with uplifted face, stilled heart, and silent lips, laid my whole being in worship at the feet of "the Lord sitting on his throne."[20]

How long I knelt there I do not know. Even immortal life seemed lost before that greatest of celestial mysteries. At length Frank, who had been silently kneeling beside me, rose and, lifting me to my feet, whispered gently, "Come."

Frank's face was pale with the depth of his emotion, and I yielded to his guidance in silence.

A long flight of low, broad steps rose from where we stood, almost to the very door of the Temple. They too were of solid pearl, bordered on either side by channels paved with golden stones through which crystal waters ran that met and mingled into one stream far out on the plain. Ascending these steps, we entered the Temple, and stood for a moment in silence. I do not know how it was, but in that brief instant—or maybe it was longer than I knew—every detail of that matchless interior was

20   1 Kings 22:19, 2 Chronicles 18:18

engraved on my memory like a photograph. In the other places I visited in heaven it had taken repeated visits to a room to enable me to describe it correctly in detail; but this, quickly as lightning flash, was stamped indelibly on me for all time—no, for eternity.

The immense dome, at that moment filled with a luminous cloud, was supported by three rows of massive pillars of gold that stood like ranks of sentries on the shining floor. The walls and floor were of pearl, as was the great platform that filled at least a third of the Temple on the eastern side. There were no seats of any kind. A railing of gold ran entirely around the platform on three sides, so that it was inaccessible from the main floor of the Temple. Beneath this railing, a pearl kneeler passed around the platform.

In the center of the platform was an immense altar of gold, supported at each corner by a golden seraph with outspread wings. Underneath it, in a great pearl basin, a fountain of sparkling water played, and I knew intuitively it was the source of the marvelous river that flowed through the gardens of heaven and washed the last stains of death and sin away from us.

Two other persons knelt with bowed heads beside the altar rail on the farther side. Four angels stood by the altar, one on each side; they were dressed in flowing garments of white, with long, slim trumpets of gold uplifted in their hands, as though waiting expectantly the signal for their trumpet call. Long draperies of silvery gossamer hung in thick folds behind the altar platform.

Suddenly we saw the draperies tremble and glow until a radiance far beyond the splendor of the sun at midday shone through them, and the whole Temple was filled with the glory of the Lord. In the midst of the luminous cloud that filled the dome, we saw the forms of angelic harpers, and as we dropped beside the altar rail with bowed heads and hid our faces from the splendor of His coming, we heard the trumpet call of the four angels around the altar, and the voices of the celestial harpers as they sang:

Holy, Holy, Holy, Lord God Almighty!
All thy works shall praise thy name,
in earth, and sky, and sea.
Holy, Holy, Holy, merciful and mighty,
God in three persons—blessed Trinity. Amen!

The voices softly drifted away, the last notes of the golden trumpets sounded, and everything was silent. We knew that the visible glory of the Lord was, for the present, withdrawn from the Temple that is His throne, but still we knelt with bowed heads in silent worship. When at last we stood I did not lift my eyes while we were still inside the Temple; I wanted the precious scene to remain in my memory as it appeared when filled with His glory.

We walked for some time in silence; I leaned on Frank's arm, for I still trembled with emotion. I was surprised that we did not return to the forest, but went still farther out onto the plain. When I saw that we approached the confluence of the two streams that issued from the fountain beneath the altar, I understood that we would return by way of the river, instead of by forest and lake.

At length we reached the stream and, stepping into a boat that lay by the shore, we were soon floating with the current toward home. We passed through incredibly beautiful scenery that I had not seen before, and which I made a mental note to visit in the future, when leisure from my daily duties permitted. Lovely villas, surrounded by beautiful grounds stretching directly up from the water's edge, lay on both sides of the river, and formed a panorama upon which the eye never tired of resting. Toward the end of the journey we passed my sister's lovely home, and we could plainly see her and her husband drinking in the scene from the window of her room.

Frank and I were both silent the greater part of the time during our journey home, observing the signs of happy domestic life which surrounded us on every side. The verandas and steps of the homes we passed were full of their happy residents; we could hear their glad voices and the merry shouts of laughter from the throngs of little children playing on the flowery lawns.

I broke our silence by saying to Frank, "I have more than once been delightfully surprised to hear the familiar songs of earth sung in heaven, but never more so than I was today. That hymn has long been a favorite of mine."

"These happy surprises do not come by chance," he replied. "One of the delights of this life is that no occasion is overlooked for reproducing here the pure enjoyments of our life on earth. It is the Father's pleasure to make us realize that this existence is but a continuance of the former life, only without its imperfections and its cares!"

"Frank, I believe you are the only one of our friends here who has never questioned me about loved ones still on earth; why is that?"

He smiled a peculiarly happy smile as he answered. "Perhaps it is because I already know more than you could tell me."

"I wondered if that was the reason," I said. I remembered well how my dear father had said, in speaking of Frank on the day of my arrival, "He stands very near to the Master"; and I knew how often he was sent on missions to the world below.

———————⌘———————

Once home, I lay down on my couch, my heart overflowing with joy and gratitude and love, beyond the power of expression; and it seemed to me the tenderness in the divine eyes that looked down upon me from the wall was deeper, purer, holier than it had been before.

"I will reach the standard of perfection You have set for me, my Savior," I faltered, with clasped hands uplifted to Him, "if it takes all my life in heaven and help from all the angels of light to accomplish it." And with these words on my lips and His tender eyes resting upon me, I sank into the blissful repose of heaven.

CHAPTER 15

So much occurred, and so rapidly, from the very hour of my entrance within the beautiful gates, that it is impossible for me to transcribe it all. I have only selected here and there a few of the incidents that happened day by day, and many things I would gladly have related have unconsciously been omitted. Of the many dear friends I met, only a very few have been mentioned, because such meetings are so similar in many respects that the constant repetition, in detail, would soon become tiresome. I have aimed principally to share incidents that would illustrate the beautiful domestic life in that happy world; to make apparent the reverence and love all hearts feel toward the blessed Trinity for every good and perfect gift; and to witness to the marvelous power of the love of Christ even in life beyond the grave.

This world, strange and new to me, held multitudes of those I loved on earth, and there was scarcely an hour that did not renew for me ties that had been severed on earth. I remember that as I was walking one day in the neighborhood of Mrs. Wickham's home, shortly after my first memorable visit there, I was attracted by an unpretentious but very beautiful house, almost hidden by luxuriant climbing rose vines, whose flowers of creamy whiteness were beyond compare with any roses I had yet seen in earth or heaven. Meeting Mrs. Wickham, I pointed to the house and asked: "Who lives there?"

"Why don't you go over and see," she suggested.

"Is it anyone I know?"

"I imagine so. See, someone is even now at the door as though expecting you."

I crossed over the snowy walk and flowery turf—for the house stood almost opposite Mrs. Wickham's, in an angle formed by two paths crossing—and before I could ascend the steps I found myself in the embrace of loving arms.

"Rebecca Sprague! I was sure it was you when I saw you go to Mrs. Wickham's a day or two ago. Didn't she tell you I was here?"

"She had no opportunity until today," I said. "But dear Aunt Ann, I would have found you soon; I am sure you know that."

"Yes, I know you would."

Then I recounted to her something of my first visit to Mrs. Wickham's. She listened with her dear face full of sympathy, then said, "There, dear, you don't need to explain. Don't I know? When the Master comes to gladden my eyes, I have no thought or care for anything beyond Him, for days and days! Oh, the joy, the peace of knowing I am safe in this blessed haven! This divine life is far greater than all our earthly dreams!"

She sat for a moment lost in thought, then said wistfully: "Now, tell me about my children—are they coming?"

I shared with her all the good news I could bring of her loved ones. We talked the hours away, recalling many sweet memories from earth— of friends and home and family ties—and looking forward to the future, when those who even the joys of heaven could not banish from our hearts would come to be with us forever.

On another evening, as the soft twilight fell and many of our home circle were gathered with us in the great flower room, we heard someone step onto the veranda, and when Frank went to the open door a gentle voice inquired, "Is Mrs. Sprague really here?"

"She is really here. Come and see for yourself."

Sweet Mary Green entered the room.

"I am so glad to welcome you home!" she said, coming to me with extended hands, her tender, earnest eyes looking into mine.

"My precious girl!" I cried, pulling her to me in a warm embrace. "I have been asking about you, and longing to see you."

"I could hardly wait to get here when I heard that you had come. Now, tell me everything!" she implored, as I drew her to a seat close beside me.

The questions asked and answers given are too sacred to retell here. Every individual member of her dear home circle was discussed, and she recounted to me many incidents that had occurred in her presence when her mother and I were together and talking of the dear child we considered far removed from us.

"I was often so close that I could have touched you with my hand, had that power been given to me," she said.

After a long, close conversation, I took her to the library, where the rest had gone to examine a new book just received that day. Confident of the welcome she would receive, I introduced her to them all as the daughter of dear friends still on earth. My youngest sister and she at once found they shared many interests and daily pursuits, and I was glad to think they would see much of each other.

There was no marking of time as we measure it on earth, although many still spoke in the language of "months" and "days" and "years." I have no way of describing it as it seemed to me then. There were periods, and allotted times; there were hours for happy duties, hours for joyful pleasures, and hours for holy praise. I only know it was all harmony, all joy, all peace, at all times and in all conditions.

CHAPTER 16

The current of my life flowed on in the heavenly way, until the months began to lengthen into years and my daily studies ascended higher in the scale of celestial mysteries. I never tired of study; much was taught and gained through the medium of observation during the journeys that I was permitted to take with my brother-in-law into different parts of the heavenly kingdom. I never lacked time for social pleasures and enjoyments, since in heaven there is no conflict of duties with inclination, no unfulfilled desires, no striving in vain for the unattainable, as in life on earth.

Many precious hours were spent in my dear parents' home, and sometimes on rare occasions I was permitted to accompany my father to his field of labor and assist him in instructing those recently arrived into the new life with little or no preparation for its duties and responsibilities. On one occasion he said to me, "I have to deal with the most difficult problem that I have ever encountered in this work: how to enlighten and help a man who suddenly plunged from an apparently honorable life into the very depths of crime. I have never been able to get him to accompany me to the river, where these earthly cobwebs would be swept from his poor brain; his excuse is always that God's mercy is so great in allowing him inside heaven's gates at all, that he is content to remain always in its lowest scale of enjoyment and life. No argument or teaching thus far can make him change his decision. He was led astray by infatuation for a strange woman, and killed his aged mother in order to steal her jewels for this wretched creature. He was executed for the crime, of which in the end he sincerely repented, but he left life with all the horror of the deed clinging to his soul."

"Has he seen his mother since coming here? Does she know of his arrival?"

"No; she is entirely alone in this world, and it was not thought wise to tell her of his coming until his soul is in a better condition to receive her. He was an only child, and does not lack the elements of refinement, but he was completely under the control of this vile woman. It is said she drugged his wine and incited him to do the dreadful deed while under its influence, because of her hatred for his mother, who opposed the woman's influence on her son. When he recovered from the influence of the wine, he was horrified at what he had done, and his infatuation for the woman turned to loathing—too late! He would not see her during his entire incarceration."

"How long was he in prison?"

"Almost a year."

"Has he seen the Christ?"

"No; he begs not to see Him. He is very repentant, and grateful to be saved from the wrath he feels was his just punishment, but though he is conscious that his sin is forgiven, he does not yet feel that he can ever stand in the presence of the Holy One. And here, as on earth, each must be willing to receive Him. His presence is never given where it is not desired. I have not yet appealed for higher help; my deep desire is to lead these weak souls upward through the strength entrusted to me. Can you suggest anything that would probably reach him?"

"His mother. May I bring her?"

He thought a moment reflectively, then said, "A woman's intuition. Yes, bring her."

I soon was on my way. I found the poor woman, laid the facts gently before her, and waited for her decision. There was no hesitation on her part; in an instant she said, "My poor boy! Certainly, I will go with you at once."

We found my father waiting for us, and went immediately to the large house where these newcomers stayed during their preparation to become full participants in the heavenly life. It was a beautiful big building in the midst of a park, with shaded walks and fountains and flowers everywhere. To one just freed from earth it would seem to be a paradise indeed; but to those of us who had tasted more of heaven's joys, something was wanting. We missed the lovely individual homes, the little children playing on the lawns, the music of the angel choir; this place was tame indeed beside the pleasures we had tasted.

We found the young man seated beneath one of the flower-laden trees, intently perusing a book that my father had left with him. There was a peaceful look on his pale face, but it was more a look of patient resignation than of fiery joy. His mother approached him alone while my father and I remained in the background. After a little time he glanced up and saw his mother standing near him. With a startled look on his face, he rose to his feet. She extended her arms toward him, and cried out pathetically, "John, my dear boy, come home to me—I need you!" That was all.

With a low cry, he knelt at her feet and clasped her knees, sobbing, "Mother! Mother!"

She stooped and put her arms around him tenderly, then drew his head gently to her breast and showered kisses on his bowed head. Oh, the warm love of a mother, the same in earth and heaven! Only the love of Christ can exceed it. Here was this wronged mother, sent into eternity by the hands of him who should have shielded and sustained her, bending above her repentant son, her motherly love for him overflowing and shining from her gentle eyes. I saw my father turn his head to conceal his emotion, and I knew that I had tears in my own eyes.

My father had explained to the mother that the first thing to be accomplished was to get her son into the river, so we now heard her say caressingly, "Come, John, my boy, take the first step upward, for your mother's sake, that in time I may have the joy of seeing you in our own home. Come with me, John."

She drew him gently, and to our great joy we saw him rise and go with her, toward the river. They walked hand in hand, and for as long as we could see them she seemed to be soothing and comforting him.

"Thank God!" my father said fervently. "There will be no further trouble now. When they return he will see with clearer vision." And so it proved.

After this, by divine permission, I became a frequent coworker with my father, and enjoyed his company and his instruction much more often than I could have done otherwise.

CHAPTER 17

One evening, some three years—counted by the calendar of earth—
after I had entered into the joys and duties of heavenly life, I
sat resting on the upper veranda of our home following a somewhat
strenuous journey to a distant city of heaven. From this part of the
veranda we caught rare glimpses of the river through the overhanging
branches of the trees; and just below us, at a little distance, we could see
the happy children at their play upon the lawn. Here Frank sought me
out, and throwing himself onto a soft veranda lounge nearby, lay for a
time motionless and silent. He looked as wearied as one can ever look
in that life, but I felt no anxiety about him, for I knew the rest would
restore him.

He had been absent on some earth mission much of the time for
many days, and I knew from experience that some of the fatigue and
care of earth could cling to us on such occasions, until we were restored
by heaven's balmy air and life-giving waters. He had not told me, as
he sometimes did, where his mission had led him, and I had not asked
him, feeling sure that he would tell me in good time the things that I
should know.

My own responsibilities had been unusual lately, leading me daily to a distant part of the heavenly kingdom, so I had not seen my loved ones on earth for a much longer period than usually elapsed between my visits. When I had last visited, all of the dear ones had seemed in such vigorous health and were so surrounded by earthly blessings that I felt they no longer needed my ministering as in the early days of their sorrow, so I had thrown all of my energies into the work assigned me by the Master.

At length, after a time of rest, my brother sat up and, after regarding me for a moment in silence, said gently, "I have news for you, little sister."

A thrill like an electric shock passed through me, and in an instant I cried out joyfully, "He is coming!"

He nodded his head, with a sympathetic smile, but did not at once reply.

"When will it be? Am I to go to him?" I asked.

He hesitated an instant before saying, "Of course you are permitted to go, but let me explain the situation before you decide."

"Oh, I must go to him! I must be the first to greet him! Perhaps he may be allowed to see me even while he is still in the flesh."

He shook his head sadly at this, and said, "No, dear; he will not know you."

"Why? Frank, tell me all—and why you think, as I plainly see you do, that it is not best I should go."

"He was apparently in perfect health, but was stricken suddenly while he worked and has not regained consciousness since. He will never awaken on earth, so your presence there could provide no comfort to him."

"When was this?"

"Three days ago; I have been with him almost constantly day and night ever since."

"Why did you not tell me sooner?"

"It was thought wise to spare you the unnecessary pain of seeing him suffer when you could not minister to him, but I have come to tell you now that you may go if you still so desire."

"He will know me as soon as his struggle is over?"

"Yes, but he will be bewildered and weak; he will need stronger help and guidance than you alone can give, and you will miss the rapture of the meeting as it would be a little later on."

"What do you think I should do? You know I will yield to your wiser judgment even against the pleadings of my heart. I can wait if that is best for him."

"I will not tell you not to go. You may accompany me if you wish. I only think that after the first bewilderment of the change has passed, after he has bathed in the waters of the River of Life, he will be better prepared for the delightful reunion that awaits him. You remember what the waters did for you, and how bewildered and oppressed in spirit you were until you went with me into the river that morning. It is the same with all of us, but where there has been serious trouble with the brain at the end of life, it is even more needed than on ordinary occasions. And that is the case with my brother; he will not be fully himself until the healing waters have swept the clouds from his brain."

"You are always right, and I will yield to your wise advice, although my heart cries out to hurry at once to his side. When will you return to him?"

"Immediately. Your wait will be short; we will be here with the morning light. My brave-hearted, wise little sister, the delay will be neither sorrowful nor long."

He stood and, bending over me, dropped a kiss lightly on my brow, and in a moment he had passed from my sight.

How strange, I thought, *that even in this matter, so near to my heart, I am able to yield uncomplainingly! Father, I thank You! I thank You for the glad reunion so soon to come; but, even more than that, for the sweet submission to You in all things that has grown into my life. Thank You that I can yield to Your will even when You would allow me to do otherwise.*

I bowed my head and gave myself up to mingled sad and happy thoughts. Was he, this dearly loved one, really insensible to his suffering? Would the Father mercifully spare him even the pain of the parting? Oh, that the morning were here! How could I wait even that brief while for the sight of his beloved face!

Suddenly I felt a soft touch on my bowed head, and a Voice I had learned to recognize and love beyond all things in earth or heaven said, "Did I not say truly that though he was dead, he will live again? What do the years of separation matter now, since the reunion is at hand? Come, and let's settle this."[21] The Master smiled down into my uplifted face. He took my extended hand into His own and sat down beside me.

"Let us consider what these years have done for you. Do you not feel that you are infinitely better prepared to confer happiness than when you parted from him you love?"

I nodded in glad affirmation.

"Do you not realize that you stand upon a higher plane, with more exalted ideas of life and its duties; and that, in the strength of the Father, you two from now on will walk upward together?"

Again I gladly agreed.

"Is the home life here less attractive than it was on earth?"

"No, no! A thousand times no!" I cried.

"Then there is nothing but joy in the reunion at hand?"

"Nothing but joy," I echoed.

Then the Savior led me to talk of the one so soon to come, and I opened my glad heart to Him and told Him of my beloved husband's

---

21   Isaiah 1:18.

noble life, unselfish toil, high aspirations, and unfaltering trustworthiness. I spoke of his fortitude in misfortune, his courage in the face of hard trials and disappointment, his forgiveness of even malicious injury, and concluded by saying, "He lived the Christianity many others professed. He always outdistanced me in that."

The face of the Master glowed as I talked, and when I finished He said, "I perceive that you have discovered the secret which makes marriage eternal as the years of heaven."

"Oh," I said, "to me marriage must be eternal! How could it be otherwise when two grow together and become as one? Death cannot separate them without destroying; they are no longer two perfect beings, but one in soul and spirit forever."[22]

"Yes," He answered, "but simply having the marriage rite pronounced does not produce this change. It is only the divinity of soul wedded to soul that can do it."

So He led me on until my soul flew upward like a lark in the early morning. He unfolded to me mysteries of the soul's life that filled my heart with rapture, but which I may not here reveal. At length, to my infinite surprise, I saw the rosy glow deepening across the sky, and knew that morning—love's morning—had dawned for me in heaven. The Master rose and, pointing to the radiance, said, "By the time you are ready to receive them they will be here." With a smile, and a touch that was a benediction, He departed.

As I rose and stood with my face uplifted to the coming day, I caught in the near distance the triumphant notes of the angels' choral song; and this morning, as though in sympathy with my thoughts, they sang, "He is risen! Hear it, you heavens, and you sons of earth! Christ is risen from the dead, and has become the firstfruits of those who have fallen asleep."[23]

---

22   Mark 10:8.

23   1 Corinthians 15:20 (NKJV).

I lifted up my voice with joy, and joined their thrilling song; and as they swept onward and the cadence drifted away, I slowly descended the stairway, crossed the lawn whose flowers never crushed or withered beneath our feet, and sank for a moment beneath the pure waters of the river. I felt no haste, no undue excitement or unrest, though I knew that the one for whom my soul had waited all these years was finally coming. The Master's presence had filled me with God's peace, which exceeds anything we can understand[24]; He had prepared and fitted me for the great happiness just ahead of me.

Uplifted with a new, strange delight, I went back across the lawn, stopping on the veranda to gather a few cream-white roses and fasten them to my robe before entering the house. Then going to the library, I refilled the golden bowl with the spicy-breathed scarlet carnations that he loved, laying one aside to fasten on my husband's shoulder. I wanted to gather the flowers that would greet him on his coming. I twisted up my hair in the manner that he had most admired, and fastened a creamy bud within the folds, that I might seem to him as I had of old.

I soon heard voices and footsteps. Yes, it was the same dear step for which I had so often listened on earth, the step that had always brought gladness to my heart, and sunshine to our home! His step in heaven! I flew to the open doorway, and in an instant was held close in the strong arms and to the loving, throbbing heart of my dear husband. What more could heaven give!

My brother, with thoughtful care, went on to the upper rooms of the house, and for a while we were alone together, we whose lives had so happily mingled, through the long years of our mortal life. I drew him into the house, and in the vestibule he again took me in his arms and drew me to his heart.

24   Philippians 4:7.

"This is heaven indeed!" he said.

We passed into the flower room, and on its threshold he stood a moment, entranced with its beauty; but when I would have related to him its history, as my brother had given it to me, he said, "Not today, my dear; I have only eyes and ears for you today; all else in heaven must wait."

So we sat and talked together as we had on earth, and the happy hours came and went, and the day melted into the twilight glow, before we realized it was half spent.

Frank had come to us around noon, and he and I together showed Will the lovely house, stood together on the broad verandas, and ate the heavenly fruit. Then we all sat together where I had spent the hours waiting in the presence of the blessed Master. I told them much of what He had said to me, and how He turned into triumphant rejoicing the hours that I had anticipated would pass in lonely waiting. The eyes of my dear husband were filled with tears, and he pressed my hand, which he still kept in his, in tender sympathy.

"Oh, darling, it is a blessed, blessed life!" I said.

"I already realize the blessedness," he replied, "for it has given me back my brother and my wife—my precious wife!"

Early the following morning I said to my husband and his brother, "We must go to your parents today. They have the first claim, after ours, Frank."

"Yes, we will go at once," they both agreed.

So together we all started. In the earliest days of my heavenly life I had sought out with much joy the home of my husband's parents, and was welcomed by them, as on earth, and given a warm place in their hearts; and we had spent many happy hours together since. Now we were taking to them a favorite son, and I realized how his coming would bring gladness to their hearts and home. It was a joyful meeting, especially for his mother, and the day was far spent before we rose to return to our own home.

"William," his mother said, fondly laying her hand on his arm and with a loving glance at me, "you had a happy home on earth—I used to think a perfect home; it will be far happier here."

"I am sure of that, Mother. I have my dear wife and Frank constantly with me; and you and my father and Josephine"—a favorite niece—"to come to here; and after awhile," he added, with a little hesitation, "the holier joys and privileges of heaven."

We turned to go, and on the threshold met an aunt who in earthly life—blind and helpless—had been a favorite with us all.

"My dear children," she exclaimed, "how good it is to see you all again!"

"Aunt Cynthia!" my husband said fondly.

"Yes, Aunt Cynthia, but no longer groping helplessly in the darkness. 'I was blind, and now I can see!'[25]" she quoted, smiling happily.

And so it was—the Master's touch had rested on her sightless eyes and, closing to the darkness of earth, they had opened upon the glories of heaven. Marvelous transition! No wonder we left her singing.

25   John 9:25.

CHAPTER 18

Days lengthened into weeks, weeks into months, which in turn crept onward into years, and the duties and joys of heaven grew clearer and dearer with each passing moment. Our home life was perfect, though we looked forward with joy to the future coming of our son and his family to make it complete. We had often spoken of going together to the great celestial sea, but the time had never seemed quite right. We knew it was one of the great mysteries of heaven, although we did not know just what to expect. One evening I said to Frank, "I have a strange desire to go to the sea, if you think it wise that we should do so."

"I am glad that want to go, because I think it is time. I was about to propose that you and my brother should take this blessed journey together."

"Won't you come with us?"

"Not this time. We will all go again together, but for now it is best that you two go alone. You know the way: through the forest that leads to the Temple, until you are almost there; then bear to the right and follow the golden path that takes you directly to the shore."

So, in the quivering light of the glorious morning we set out, full of a holy joy that we might take this special journey together. We entered and traversed the great forest, where the golden light fell through the quivering branches overhead, and birds of gorgeous plumage and thrilling song were darting everywhere. We heard, nearer and nearer, the regular dashing of the waves against the shore, and then bursts of triumphant song and the harmony of many musical instruments. At length we emerged from the forest, and stood mute and motionless before the overwhelming glory of the scene before us.

Can I describe it as it appeared to me that day? Never, until my lips can speak, and your heart understand, the language of the royal courts above. At our feet, a golden shore many hundred feet wide sloped down toward the water, extending on either hand far beyond the limits of our vision. It caught and radiated the morning light until wherever it was visible it glittered and glimmered like the dust of diamonds and other precious stones, and the waves, as they came and went in ceaseless motion, caught up the sparking sand and carried it on their crests, like the phosphorescence we sometimes see in the wake of a vessel in mid ocean.

And the sea! It spread out before us in a radiance that passes description in any language I have ever known. It was like the white glory that shone through the windows of the Temple, and beneath this shining glory we could see in the roll of the waves the blue tint of the waters of that sea which has no limit to its depths or bounds. Upon its shining surface we saw in every direction boats, representing all nations of the earth, but in beauty of construction far surpassing anything earth has ever known. They were like great open pleasure barges, and were filled with people looking eagerly toward the shore, many in their eagerness standing erect and gazing with wistful, expectant eyes into the faces of those waiting there.

Ah, the people upon the shore! Numberless as the sands of the sea, they stood far as the eye could reach, along the shore of that infinite sea, a great mass of beautiful souls clad in the spotless garments of the redeemed. Many among them had golden harps and various instruments of music, and whenever a boat touched the shore and its passengers were welcomed by the glad voices and tender embraces of their loved ones in the throng, the harps would he held aloft, all of the golden instruments would sound, and the vast multitude would break forth into a triumphant song of victory over death and the grave.

"Do these people always stand here?" I wondered softly.

"Not the same people," said a radiant being person near us, who had heard my question. "But there is always a throng of people here—those who are expecting friends from the other life, and those who assemble to share their joy. Some of the heavenly singers also are always here, but not always the same ones. You will notice that most of those who arrive are led quietly away by their friends, and many others are constantly joining the multitude."

He moved on toward the shore, and left us surveying the scene below in awe and wonder.

We soon became deeply interested in watching the reunions, and found ourselves joining with rapture in the glad songs of rejoicing. Now and then a face we remembered seeing on earth would be among the eager faces in the boats, but none that had been especially dear to us; still it made us notice more closely and sympathize more heartily with those who welcomed beloved friends. Now we would see a wife caught in the close embrace of a waiting husband; or a little child would spring with a glad cry into the outstretched arms of the happy mother; friend would clasp friend in glad reunion; and an aged mother would be folded to the heart of a beloved child.

As one boat of more than usual strength and beauty came riding gracefully over the waves, we observed the tall figure of a man standing near her prow with his arms about a graceful woman who stood by his side. Each shaded their dazzled eyes from the unaccustomed splendor with an uplifted hand and scanned, wistfully and searchingly, the faces of the crowd as the boat neared the shore. Suddenly with a great thrill of joy surging through my being, I cried out, "It is our precious son, and his dear wife! And they have come together!"

In an instant we were swiftly moving through the throng that parted in ready sympathy to let us pass. And, as the boat touched the shore, they quickly came to us—the dear daughter already clasped close by her own happy parents who were waiting near the water's edge, while at the same instant we felt the arms of our beloved son enfolding us; and soon we were all embracing. Oh, what a rapturous moment that was! Our home life in heaven complete, no partings forever!

As we stood with joined arms, scarcely realizing the unexpected bliss, the heavenly choir broke into song; and with uplifted faces radiant with joy, eyes filled with happy tears and voices trembling with emotion, we all joined in the glad anthem:

> Glory be unto the Father, and to the Son!
> Glory be unto the ever-blessed Three in One!
> No more sorrow, no more parting, no more grief or pain;
> Christ has broken death's strong fetters, we are free again.
> Heart to heart and hand to hand,
> meet we on the golden strand.
> Glory, glory to the Father! Glory to the Son!
> Glory be unto the ever-blessed Three in One!
> Alleluia! Amen!

The song rose and swelled triumphantly as the vast multitude caught it up, and the surge of the waves made a deep undertone to the melody that increased its solemnity, as with bowed heads and full hearts we left hand in hand; and the light that fell about us was purer, holier, more divine, than it had ever been before.

CHAPTER 19

A time came when one day as I stood in my lovely room that had really become to me a shrine, and looked up into the pictured face of the Christ above me, I fancied that the tender eyes looking down into mine no longer told of an eternal love alone, but carried in their depths also a pity, a loving compassion which I had never noticed there before. Then as I turned toward my couch I even fancied that His hands reached out from the canvas and rested in benediction on my head. I stood a moment in blessed peace before Him, then as the hands seemed to be withdrawn, I turned and lay down for a moment's rest.

Strange thoughts and fancies crept into my brain, such as I had not known in years. I felt confused and bewildered, and started up restlessly from my pillow, only to fall back again in doubt, and something like dread. What could it mean? How could the old unrest of earth find a place in this divine retreat?

Then I heard unfamiliar voices. Someone said, "Her color is better than it has been for several days, I think."

"Yes, there is no doubt that she is better today. There is really hope for her now, I am sure. But she came very near passing through the Gates."

"Very near passing through the Gates"! As though I had not passed through, and in returning left them so ajar that gleams of the heavenly radiance from beyond them will fall about my life forever!

I have been in my Father's house.

And now I can answer with confidence the question posed by the familiar hymn. We *shall* know each other there!

AUTHOR'S NOTE

In the many letters received since the publication of *Intra Muros*, repeated inquiries have been made of me about different points contained in the book, and it has been suggested that possibly the addition of a few pages, as a supplement to the book, might explain some matters or, possibly, make more clear some points that have not been fully comprehended by the reader.

Let me in the beginning reassert what I have said before: I have never claimed that this strange experience is either a revelation or an inspiration. It came to me during a period when I was overcome by great physical suffering, and I have always considered it as being sent in compensation for that suffering. Be that as it may, the experience has been a great comfort and help to me and, through the letters received from others, I am led to believe it has been the same to many who have read it, for which I am extremely gratified. I wish that I might give the entire experience just as it came to me, but I find that the language of earth is wholly inadequate for me to do so. There were so many mysteries, so many teachings far beyond anything that we know in this life—I find myself bewildered and lost when I attempt to convey to others the marvelous things which at that time seemed to me to be a most wonderful revelation.

The question has repeatedly been asked me, "Was this a real experience, or merely an imaginative story?" What I have written above will as nearly answer that question as it is possible for me to do. The preface and text are as nearly accurate as I can make them; and anything that I might add on that point would simply be superfluous. To me, at the time, it was as real as any experience in this life could possibly be.

Questions have been asked respecting the comparative distances in heaven and our powers of passing from one point to another; and I have even been asked if in the other life we developed wings that aided us in passage, like the wings of a bird. These matter-of-fact questions are sometimes quite difficult to answer, for my belief is, that if I were really in the other life, as during this experience I seemed to be, my thoughts would be so far above, so lifted beyond such temporal matters, that I would be unable to answer questions like these satisfactorily on my return to this life.

Looking back on it now, and trying to gather facts from the impressions that I received then, I should say that none who have ever passed through mortal life would in any way be changed from their present personal appearance, except to be etherealized and glorified. When I seemed to stand in that wonderful Temple filled with the glory of God the Father, four angels with uplifted trumpets stood beside the golden altar on the great platform of pearl, and from their shoulders shadowy pinions enfolded them and touched the floor upon which they stood. And when, in a moment of bewildering emotion, I lifted my eyes to the formerly cloud-filled dome, I saw around the members of the hitherto invisible choir, the shadowy pinions of which we so often read, half concealing their harps and instruments of gold. Also, at the close of that wonderful day when I had first met the Savior, when we heard the angel voices as we stood together in the great flower room, and, looking upward, saw the child faces in the golden twilight above us, they too had delicate shadowy wings, half concealing the baby forms. Except for this, I have no recollection of having seen any of those glorious wings of which we so often read.

To me it seems that to the angels of God who have always lived in heaven, wings are given; but to us who have suffered and toiled and borne the cross below, is given only the glorified form, such as our Savior himself bore. We appear to our friends when we meet them over there just as we did when they saw us here, only purified and perfect. Still, we had powers of locomotion given us that carried us from point to point swiftly and securely, as though borne by a boat upon the waters.

I do not know how I can better illustrate this point than by sharing a little incident not mentioned in the book. I remember, as I sat one morning upon the upper terrace in the home of my sister whom I had welcomed there soon after my arrival (and who, though really then a resident of earth, has since passed over and taken possession of that beautiful home prepared for her), that my sister said to me, "I often look across the river to those lovely hills in the distance, and wonder if it is all as beautiful there as here. I mean some day to go and see."

"Why not go today?" I suggested.

"Could you go with me this morning?" she asked, as she turned her radiant face again toward the river and the lovely fields beyond.

"With pleasure," I replied. "I have often wished to go myself. There is something very inviting in the beautiful landscape beyond the river. Where is Oliver?" I asked. "Would he like to join us?"

"No," she said, looking smilingly toward me, "he has gone on an important mission for the Master today; but you and I can go, and be at home again before his return."

"Then let's do so," I replied, rising and giving her my hand.

She stood at once and, instead of turning toward the stairway in the center of the building, we turned and walked deliberately to the low wall that surrounded the upper veranda. Without a moment's hesitation we stepped over this into the sweet air that lay around us. There was no more fear of falling than if our feet had been on solid ground. We had the power of passing through the air at will, and through the water, just as we had the power of walking on the crystal paths and grass.

We ascended slightly until we were just above the treetops, and then—how can I describe it?—we did not fly, we made no effort either with our hands or our feet; I can only think of the word "drifting" to describe at all this wonderful experience. We went as a leaf or a feather floats through the air on a balmy day, and the sensation was most delightful. We saw beneath us through the green branches of the trees little children playing, and people walking—some for pleasure, some for duty. As we neared the river we looked down at the pleasure boats on the water and at the people sitting or lying or walking beneath it, on the pebbly bottom; and we saw them with the same distinctness as though we were looking at them simply through the atmosphere.

Conversing as we drifted onward, we soon were over the tops of the hills to which we had looked so longingly from the veranda of my sister's house, and, for some time, we had no words to exchange; our hearts were filled with sensations such as only the scenes of heaven can give. Then my sister said very softly, quoting from one of the old earth hymns, "'Sweet fields beyond the swelling flood stand dressed in living green.'"

And in the same spirit, I answered, "'It is indeed a rapturous scene that rises to our sight; sweet fields arrayed in living green, and rivers of delight.'"

As we passed on, looking down we began to see many suburban villages, similar to that in which our own happy homes were situated.

Among many of them there was an unfamiliar air, and the architecture of the buildings in many respects seemed quite different from our own. I suggested to my sister that we drop downward a little. On doing so, we soon realized what caused this apparent difference in style and surroundings. Where our homes were situated we were surrounded by people we had known and loved on earth, of our own nationality. Many of the villages over which we were now passing we found were home to people who, to us, would be termed of foreign nations, and each village retained some of the peculiarities of its earthly style, which, to us, were naturally unfamiliar. We recognized again the wisdom and goodness of the Father in thus allowing friends of the same nationality to be located near each other in heaven, as on earth.

Still drifting, we passed over an exquisitely beautiful valley, between low hills of the most enchanting greenery, where we saw a group of people seated on the ground in a semicircle. They seemed to be hundreds in number, and in their midst a man was standing who, apparently, was talking to them. Something familiar, and yet unfamiliar, in the scene attracted us, and I said, "Let's go nearer, and hear, if possible, what he is saying, and see who these people are."

Upon doing this we found the people to resemble in a great measure our own Indian tribes; their dress, though like what they would have worn on earth, was so etherealized as to be surpassingly beautiful. But the dusky faces and the long black hair still remained. The faces, with intense interest depicted on each, were turned toward the man who, we could see, was talking to them, and, looking upon him, we saw at once that he belonged to the Anglo-Saxon race. In a whisper of surprise I said to my sister, "Why, he is a missionary!"

As so often seemed to happen there, when a surprise or a difficulty presented itself, there was always someone near to answer and enlighten us. And so we found on this occasion that our instructor was beside us ready to answer any surprise or question that might be asked. He said at once:

"Yes, you are right. This is a missionary who gave his life to what on earth were called the heathen. He spent many years working with them and enlightening those who sat in darkness, with the result, as you see before you, of bringing hundreds into the kingdom of the Master. But, as you will naturally suppose, they have much to learn, and here he still gathers them about him, and day by day leads them higher and higher into the blessed life"

"Are there many like him," I asked, "doing this work here?"

"Many hundreds," he said. "To these poor minds, unenlightened as they were when they first came, heaven is as beautiful and happy a place as it is to any who have ascended higher, simply because we can enjoy only in the capacity to which our souls can reach. There are none of us who do not still have much to learn of this wonderful place."

In several instances, as we drifted above the villages, we heard songs of praise rising from people gathered below. In many cases, to our surprise, the hymns and the words were those with which we had been familiar on earth, and, although sung in a strange tongue, we understood them all. That was another of the wonderful surprises of heaven: there was no language there that we could not understand.

On and on and on, through wonderful scenes of beauty, we passed, returning finally to our own homes by a different way from that by which we had gone forth, seeming to have made almost a circle in our pleasant journeying. When I left my sister in her own home she whispered to me as she said good-bye for the present, "It has been a day of such wonderful rest and pleasure that we must soon repeat it together."

And I answered, "Yes, dear, we will."

In several instances the subject of dual marriages has been introduced. More than once it has been asked, "If a man marries in early life and is devotedly attached to the woman he has married, but unfortunately loses her, and after many years of solitary waiting finds another congenial soul to whom his whole heart goes out and marriage is the result and they have many years of wedded happiness together before she too is called home, to whom will he belong in the other life?"

In the many phases of the divine life that seemed to come to me in my vision, questions such as the above were never by any means suggested. Speaking from my own natural intuitions, I think that as soon as the immortal part of us leaves the earthly dwelling, it lays down forever all thoughts that embarrassed or grieved or pained the spirit. In the homes of heaven there was perpetual love and joy and peace and happiness without measure. This one thing I know: in heaven there are no conflicting ties, no questions that distress, no conditions that annoy; the whole heart springs up to do the will of the Father, and nothing less than that will suffice.

In answer to the question many times proposed to me, about whether I consider this experience as a revelation, I can only repeat, that I wrote it as it came to me, and each reader must draw his own conclusion concerning it. I can be the guide for no one.

I am aware of some seeming inconsistencies in the book. Looking back on it after nearly four years have passed, it seems to me to be more a series of instructions such as we give little children here in a kindergarten. It does not purport to be a revelation of what has been or what will be, in the strict sense of the word, but, as I have already suggested, more as we would teach children.

I noticed, in transcribing this strange experience, the fact that the lesson to be taught almost invariably came first as an illustration; after my wonder and pleasure had taken in all that the picture itself had to teach, then followed the revelation, or a general application of its meaning. For instance, to make my meaning more clear:

When I first entered heaven's gates, I was shown the wonders of the celestial gardens and the magic of the beautiful river, then came the meeting with loved ones from whom I had been so long separated. And so I came to know the rapture of the disembodied spirit on its first entrance "within the walls." Afterward followed the instruction or first lessons concerning this life into which I seemed to have entered, until, as I said, the first illustrations and the instructions formed for me one perfect lesson.

When, as time passed, I met and welcomed my dear sister, my husband, and my son, I experienced the other side of the equation—the joy that came even to the angels in heaven when they welcomed the beloved ones who came to them from the world below. And so, all through the book, the instruction was invariably preceded by the illustration; therefore, I can only think, if any meaning can be attached to this strange vision, that it is simply a lesson in a general way of what we may expect and hope for when *we* reach the other shore.

The question is many times repeated, "Does this experience retain its vividness as time passes, or does it grow unreal and dreamlike to you?"

I can partially forget even some of the happiest experiences of my earthly life, but time seems only to intensify to me the wonders of those days when my feet really stood in the borderland of the two worlds. It seemed to me that with every step we took in the divine life our souls reached up toward something better, and we had no inclination to look behind to that which had passed, or to try to solve what in our mortal life had been intricate or perplexing questions or mysteries. Like the cup that is filled to overflowing at the fountain with pure and sparkling water, so our souls were filled—more than filled—from the fountain of all good, until there was no longer room for anything else.

"How then," you may ask, "could you reach out for more, when you had all that you could receive?" Because moment by moment, hour by hour, our souls grew and expanded and opened to receive fresh courses of the divine instruction that was constantly lifting us nearer to the source of all perfection.

Some of the letters that have come to me have been so heartbreaking that they have called forth sympathetic tears, and an intense longing to speak with authority on the questions raised. God has not given me that privilege; I can only tell how it seemed to me in those blissful hours when earth seemed remote and heaven very near and real.

One suffering mother writes, "Do you think I could pray still for my darling girl?" How I longed to take her in sympathetic arms and whisper to her that I did not doubt that the dear child she loved was praising God continually and no longer had need of earthly prayer. She loved and trusted the Savior as she went down into the valley of shadows, and His loving arms received and comforted her.

To all such questions (and I received many letters like this) I would say: "Look up, dear friends, and see the loved ones, as I saw those so dear to me, happy and blessed beyond all human conception in the home of many mansions prepared for us by our loving Father." Oh, those wonderful mansions upon which my longing heart looks back! Believe in them, look forward to them, beloved friends, for we have the Savior's promise that they are there: "In My Father's house are many mansions."[26] His promises never fail, and I am sure of one thing: they will not be less

---

26   John 14:2 (NKJV).

beautiful than those I saw in my vision.

This thought, to me, answers in a measure the questions asked in regard to dual marriages. My own belief of this mortal life is, that no two friends can occupy the same place in our hearts. Each heart is filled with welcoming rooms, and to each beloved guest a room is assigned exclusively for himself. That room is always his. If death, or distance, or even disgrace, separates him from us, still the room is his and his only forever. No other person can ever occupy it. Others may have rooms equally choice, but when a guest has once departed from the room he has held in another's heart, the door of that room is barred forever; it is set aside—a place reserved for the departed guest. And so, in heaven, each guest has his separate room or home. "My Father's house has many rooms . . . I am going there to prepare a place [room] for you."[27]

I am no advocate of second marriages. The thought of two lives coming together as one is beautiful to me; but nevertheless, I do not believe that a man sins against the memory of a beloved wife who has died, when he places by her side (not in her place) a good woman to cheer and brighten his home. That woman could not, even if she wanted, take the place left vacant in his home and heart; it is a room set aside for its own occupant. I speak, of course, of true marriages, where not only hands are joined, but hearts and souls are knit together as one forever.

"What are the duties of heaven?"

They are so many and varied, I should judge, as to make the question unanswerable. Much in *Intra Muros* shows the pattern of daily life there.

27   John 14:2 (NIV).

"What about rest?"

Rest is one of the duties as well as the pleasures of heaven. Rest does not of necessity mean inactivity. How often in this life does laying aside of one duty and taking up another bring rest to both mind and body! Still, as I found it, there was at times absolute "rest" for both mind and body in that blissful repose that only heaven can give.

———————— ✐ ————————

In only one instance of the many letters I received was any feeling produced in their perusal except that of pleasure and gratitude that I—with so little physical strength of my own—could bring comfort and pleasure into the lives of others. I thank our gracious Father that he has so kindly permitted it. The one letter to which I refer contains so many almost puerile inquiries, that I simply laid it aside with a quotation from St. Paul, "of the earth earthly," and asked the Father to lift the heart of the writer into a purer light.

In conclusion I can only reiterate that I am not a prophet, nor a seer; but, in my inmost soul, I honestly believe that if the joys of heaven are greater, if the glories *Within the Walls* are more radiant than I in my vision beheld them, I cannot understand how even the immortal spirit can bear to look upon them.

R. R. S.

HOW DO I GET TO HEAVEN?

From Pastor Steve Berger

S urely this question comes to mind after reading Rebecca Springer's account. Let me share with you how you too can be a part of this paradise, this special place, called heaven. Scripture tells us that the entrance to heaven is for those who are saved.[28] But how is one saved?

God wants you to know Him and experience His amazing love for you, but before that can happen, you must make a decision. Most of the time, we don't like to make serious decisions. In our society being lukewarm is comfortable and popular. In this middle ground, everyone's okay and no one has to take a stand or make bold commitments. Lukewarm choices are usually based on personal pleasure and popular opinion, rarely on God's truth.

That's why God commands us to live boldly. He beckons us out of the lukewarm middle where we're undecided. Jesus said, "He who is not with Me is against Me, and he who does not gather with Me scatters

---

28   John 3:5, 18, 21.

abroad."[29] He's very clear. Jesus cuts through people's opinions and asks you to make a decision. There is no such thing as a closet Christian.

Fact #1: Death Is Inevitable

King David wrote, "Indeed, You have made my days as handbreadths, and my age is as nothing before You; certainly every man at his best state is but vapor."[30] David referred to handbreadths, which is just the width of the palm of your hand. He described life as a vapor, meaning something that passes quickly. Our lives, in God's eyes, are no wider than the palm of our hands and pass very quickly like a vapor. Death is inevitable. We're not invincible.

James wrote in the New Testament, "How do you know what your life will be like tomorrow? Your life is like the morning fog—it's here a little while, then it's gone."[31] We don't know what will happen tomorrow, or even in the next moment. Therefore we must be prepared today. Sarah and I have peace, comfort, and hope that comes from the fact that our son Josiah made the bold decision to trust Christ as his Savior, so he was ready to meet Jesus. Jesus has given him eternal life.

Have you prepared for your own mortality? You must make a decision in advance, because it's too late to make it after your death.

Fact #2: Heaven Isn't Automatic

Heaven isn't everyone's default destination, contrary to popular opinion. When death happens, we like to say, "That person is in a better place" . . . but are we really sure?

29   Matthew 12:30 (NKJV).
30   Psalm 39:5 (NKJV).
31   James 4:14.

The absolute truth must come from God's Word, not people's opinions.

The apostle Paul wrote in the New Testament in Galatians 5:19–21:

The works of the flesh are evident, which are: adultery, fornication, uncleanness, lewdness, idolatry, sorcery, hatred, contentions, jealousies, outbursts of wrath, selfish ambitions, dissensions, heresies, envy, murders, drunkenness, revelries, and the like; of which I tell you beforehand, just as I also told you in time past, that those who practice such things will not inherit the kingdom of God.

Paul is saying that you cannot live a life of sin, rejecting Christ and His solution for your sin, and then expect to spend eternity in the Kingdom of God. It simply doesn't work that way.

We all must prepare for eternity by saying yes to Christ and living a life that reflects that decision. There are no guarantees without making that decision.

It is clear from God's Word that sinfulness and sinners will never enter heaven. Only those written in the Lamb's Book of Life (people who have said yes to Jesus) will be granted access.

Fact #3: Hell Is Real

Jesus talked more about hell than all the other prophets combined. It was an important topic to Him; He wanted people to know the consequences of their decisions. In Luke 16:19–31 Jesus talked about a poor man, Lazarus, who went to heaven and a rich man who went to hell. The story was contrary to traditional Jewish thinking. Most listeners would have thought, *Isn't it obvious that the rich man would automatically go to heaven?*

Jesus tells us that the rich man was "in torments in Hades."

Hell is a literal place of torment for those who consciously and willingly reject the matchless, sacrificial love of God found in Jesus Christ. Hell is not a state of being; it's not a metaphor; it's not a symbol. Hell is a real place. The people who are in hell are in torment because they could have said yes, but they said no to God's free gift of eternal life for their entire lives.

It's too late to make the decision when you're in hell. You must cry out for God's love and mercy on this side of eternity.

C. S. Lewis put it this way: "A man can't be *taken* to hell, or *sent* to hell: you can only get there on your own steam."[32] In order to go to hell, you have to walk over the sacrificial love that Jesus poured out for us on the cross. You have to willingly say no to God's salvation, and guess what? His salvation is the one thing that can keep you out of hell. Listen, when someone ends up in hell, it is God giving them for all eternity exactly what they wanted—a life without God and His goodness . . . forever.

Fact #4: God Loves You

Yes, God loves *you*, with all your sin and baggage and wounds and addictions and doubts. Yes, *you*, with all your stuff . . . God loves *you*! He loves you in spite of all you've done.

You need Him, He knows it, and that's why God sent Jesus. He knows everything about you, and His greatest desire is to take your sinfulness and brokenness, and love you into a place of healing and redemption. God says, "When life on this earth is over, I want to love you for all eternity in heaven, where there is no more sin, suffering, or brokenness."

---

32   C. S. Lewis, *The Dark Tower & Other Stories* (New York: Harcourt Brace Jovanovich, 1977), 49.

Yes, God loves you, with all your sin and baggage and wounds and addictions and doubts.

Romans 5:8 says, "God demonstrates His own love toward us, *in that while we were still sinners, Christ died for us*" (NKJV, emphasis mine). God loves you so much that He didn't even wait for you to clean up your act before He sent Jesus to take the penalty of your sin and die in your place. God didn't just talk about love—He demonstrated it. God's demonstrated love hung on a cross for *you*—and He did it while you hated and rejected Him. Now that's love! It's love in action, not a philosophy.

So what are you waiting for? It doesn't matter what you've done in the past—let it be your past and start a new life in Christ today. God loves you so much that He sent Jesus to die for you while you were still a sinner. God loves you so much that He's waiting for you, in your true home, and He offers you true and eternal hope.

Fact #5: You Must Be Born Again

It's not about religion—it's about new birth. John 3 records Jesus' conversation about eternal life with a very religious man named Nicodemus. He said this: "Most assuredly, I say to you, unless one is born again, he cannot see the kingdom of God. . . . Do not marvel that I said to you, 'You must be born again.'"[33]

Nicodemus was a good man; he lived a "religious" life. He tried hard to keep the Ten Commandments, yet he fell short, like all of us do. Jesus essentially told him, "It's not about religion—it's about being born again in order to live in the Kingdom of God forever."

33   John 3:3, 7 NKJV.

You must be born again. It's not a bumper sticker or just a saying. It's reality, and it's necessary so that you can have an abundant life on earth and eternal life in heaven.

How to Be Born Again

Jesus said in the gospel of Mark, "The time is fulfilled, and the kingdom of God is at hand. Repent, and believe in the gospel."[34]

Repent. To repent means to change your mind and change your direction, to quit running from God and run toward God instead. Acts 17:30 says, "Truly, these times of ignorance God overlooked, but now commands all men everywhere to repent." You must repent.

Believe in the gospel. Believe Jesus rose from the dead. Believe the Good News that Jesus came to pay the price for all of your sins (past, present, and future). Believe and trust that Jesus died in your place because God loves *you*.

Receive Christ. John 1:12 says, "As many as received Him, to them He gave the right to become children of God, to those who believe in His name." Receiving Christ is something you do as an act of your own will through prayer.

---

34   Mark 1:15 NKJV.

Your Prayer of Decision

If you are ready to make this decision for Christ, simply tell Him. Tell Him you want to repent. Tell Him you want to turn away from your past and run to Him. Tell Him you believe in the gospel—you know Jesus paid the price for your sins and you believe in Him. Receive Jesus. Invite Him into every part of your life to heal you, to restore you, to break your bondage to sin, and to open your heart to His love and gift of eternal life.

WHAT SCRIPTURE TELLS US ABOUT HEAVEN

Scripture tells us what heaven is.

Scripture	What *Is* in Heaven
Matthew 8:11 and Luke 12:37	We will have fellowship and communion with both old friends and new.
Matthew 5:11–12	There will be rewards in heaven.
Luke 15:7, 10	There will be joy in heaven.
Luke 16:19–25	There will be peace in heaven.
John 14:2–3	Jesus is preparing a special place for us.
1 Corinthians 2:9–10	We will not understand all the things of God. He's supernatural, omnipotent, omniscient and omnipresent. In time the Holy Spirit will reveal the deep things.

Scripture	What *Is* in Heaven
1 Corinthians 13:12	We will see God face-to-face. We will know, even as we are known. We will know things completely, because we are completely known by God.
1 Corinthians 15:40–45	We are raised in incorruption, glory and power. We are raised in a supernatural, spiritual body as a living spirit.
Philippians 3:20–21	Our resurrected bodies will be transformed to be like Jesus' glorious body. How fun will that be?
2 Timothy 4:8 and Revelation 2:10	We will have crowns—the crown of righteousness for loving His appearing and the crown of life for being faithful until death. All is recognized, remembered, and rewarded in heaven.
Hebrews 11:16	God has prepared a special city.
2 Peter 3:13	There will be righteousness in heaven and we are called to look to the new heaven and new earth and live on this earth with a heavenly focus.
1 John 3:2	To see God, we'll need to be like Him, and we cannot do that in our current, corrupt bodies. Our heavenly bodies will have capabilities far beyond anything we can imagine.

Scripture	What *Is* in Heaven
Revelation 3:12	We will be pillars in God's temple. A pillar represents strength, security, and stability. We will be rock solid in our relationship with God.
Revelation 7:15	We will be serving in heaven.
Revelation 14:13	There will be rest in heaven.
Revelation 21:7	We will inherit all things from the Creator of the universe through our intimate Father/child relationship with Him. Can you imagine the inheritance from almighty God?
Revelation 22:1–2	There will be water of life, a tree of life, and healing leaves for God's people to experience. Life and healing will abound.
Revelation 22:5	We will rule and reign forever as kings and priests to our God. We will serve and worship Him without hindrance, obstacle, or hassle—forever.
Revelation 22:12	We will have rewards. We'll be rewarded according to our works. Remember, every Kingdom-expanding act is remembered and rewarded in heaven.

Scripture also tells us what heaven is not.

Scripture	What Is *Not* in Heaven
Luke 20:36	There is no death in heaven.
Revelation 7:17	There is no sorrow in heaven.
Revelation 20:10	The devil and his demons are not in heaven. Satan's deceptive works are not there.
Revelation 21:4; Isaiah 65:19	There will be no tears in heaven. God will wipe away every one of them. There will be no death, pain, or sorrow.
Revelation 21:8	Murder, sexual immorality, pornography, sorcery, drug addiction, and witchcraft are not in heaven. Every evil thing that these sins create is completely gone and absent from heaven.
Revelation 21:23–25	There's no darkness in heaven. God illuminates heaven with His glory.
Revelation 21:27	There is no sin in heaven. Nothing enters heaven that will defile, contaminate, or pollute it. Nothing is in heaven that doesn't reflect the perfection of God.
Revelation 22:3	There's no more curse in heaven. Think about it. Every byproduct of the Fall is nonexistent.
Revelation 22:5	There will be no more night.

There are also comforting Scriptures that help us through our grief when someone goes to heaven:

Romans 14:8	Psalm 116:15	1 Thessalonians 5:9–10
Revelation 21:4	Psalm 23:4	John 14:1–6
Matthew 5:4	1 Corinthians 16:13	Proverbs 18:10
Psalm 42:10	Isaiah 51:11	2 Samuel 12:21–23